LIVING OFF THE GRID

LIVING OFF THE GRID:
A SIMPLE GUIDE TO CREATING AND MAINTAINING A SELF-RELIANT SUPPLY OF ENERGY, WATER, SHELTER, AND MORE

Dave Black

Skyhorse Publishing

Skyhorse Publishing books may be purchased in bulk at special discounts for sales promotion, corporate gifts, fund-raising, or educational purposes. Special editions can also be created to specifications. For details, contact the Special Sales Department, Skyhorse Publishing, 307 West 36th Street, 11th Floor, New York, NY 10018 or info@skyhorsepublishing.com.

Skyhorse® and Skyhorse Publishing® are registered trademarks of Skyhorse Publishing, Inc.® , a Delaware corporation.

Visit our website at www.skyhorsepublishing.com.

10 9 8 7 6 5 4 3 2 1

Library of Congress Cataloging-in-Publication Data
Black, David S.

   Living off the grid : a simple guide to creating and maintaining a self reliant supply of energy, water, shelter, and more / By Dave Black.
       p. cm.
   ISBN 978-1-60239-316-5 (alk. paper)
   1.   Sustainable living. 2. Energy conservation. 3. Ecological houses. 4. Water conservation. 5. Waste minimization. I. Title. II. Title: Guide to a self reliant supply of energy, water, shelter, and more.

   GF78.B57 2008
   640—dc22   2008038004

Printed in Canada

Contents

Epigraph

Aunty Entity: *We call it Underworld. That's where Bartertown gets its energy.*
Max: *What, oil? Natural gas?*
Aunty Entity: *Pigs.*
Max: *You mean pigs like those?*
Aunty Entity: *That's right.*
Max: *Bullshit!*
Aunty Entity: *No. Pig shit.*
Max: *What?*
The Collector: *Pig shit. The lights, the motors, the vehicles, all run by a high-powered gas called methane. And methane cometh from pig shit.*

—From *Mad Max Beyond Thunderdome*

Introduction

I've always been impressed by the ability of some people to adapt to less-than-perfect conditions. When I say less than perfect, I'm not talking about missing the family's favorite TV show because of a blown fuse during a rainstorm, or the fact that a casserole's been left in the oven too long and burned. I'm talking about real annoyances like no electric utility, no running water, no hot water, no toilet to sit on or shower to take. No TV, no computer, no air conditioner. No supermarket for hundreds of miles, and no transportation to get to it.

It's been nearly forty years since I first left affluent America and found myself immersed in this type of environment. Suddenly I was part of an Andean culture in which the everyday luxuries of the modern twentieth-century household were completely absent. It was a return to an eighteenth-century lifestyle, and an austere one even by those standards. For all intents and purposes the people I lived among were devoid of any appreciable knowledge of modern luxuries like TVs and electric refrigerators and such, and I found the old adage "ignorance is bliss" to be an accurate summary of the resulting psychology. Of course, they still struggled with the same problems we all face—family arguments, abusive relationships, alcoholism, illness, and injury—but life was lived at a slower, more relaxed pace, and the neuroses of keeping up with the Joneses were practically nonexistent. It was only when these people got a glimpse of modern luxuries, or when somebody managed to obtain some—or when somebody from outside the community (usually a white missionary or humanitarian worker) moved in and rented a structure that they then modified with the latest amenities—that the Andean people realized they lacked these items. This awareness inevitably led to envy, envy to an insatiable drive to "get" things, and possessing these "things" to a neurotic feeling of dissatisfaction and resentment.

Twenty years later I was in Saudi Arabia, exploring caves beneath the Dahna dunes. A Bedouin family had noticed our activity. In traditional Bedouin style they were friendly, and in this remote part of Saudi, away from the religious restrictions of the urbanized Saudis who had long ago turned away from the Bedouin lifestyle, the family had sent their daughter, a beautiful young unveiled woman in a bright silk blouse, to invite us to their encampment for tea. In this part of the world a social invitation of this type to total strangers implied great trust in human nature and a noble pride in Bedouin traditions. To turn down the invitation would have been a horrible insult, so we accompanied the young woman to the encampment a few dunes over from our cave. Here I found the same unawareness of "things" that I had found in the Andes two decades before. There were some tents with carpet floors, one of which housed a cooking area with a single-burner stove that used gasoline. The only ties to modernity and the grid were their tiny white Toyota truck and a generator that ran a single incandescent light in the main tent on special occasions. When I returned to the area in 2005 and 2006, there was a whole new attitude. The race for possessions was on. Even in remote Bedouin camps located in the desert wasteland, there were satellite dishes driving TVs, cell phones, refrigerators, and many other indications of a simple people headed for total dependence on the modern grid.

Now in many places in the world, generally the more affluent places, there's a drive to return to a state of independence from the grid systems. And that's what strikes me as being so humorous about the green trend. Half the world is trying to get on the grid while the other half is trying to get off.

When I wrote this book I had been a resident of San Juan County, Utah, off and on for eight years. San Juan has been called the "most conservative county in the most conservative state in the nation," and it can't be far from the truth. Here's an area where because of its climate and altitude the potential for using solar and wind energy is extraordinary, yet the two resources go virtually untapped simply because of the stigma of being "green." Any recommendation by the federal or state governments or by conservationist groups to decrease the use of finite fuels by switching to a greater percentage of renewable sources of energy is met with loathing and distrust, and is patently labeled by local politicians and press as a scam run by liberals and groups like the Sierra Club and the Southern Utah Wilderness Alliance to usurp the rights of locals. Even in the face of the war in Iraq and the enormous gas price increases of 2008, it apparently doesn't even occur to these people that a decreased reliance on a fossil fuel–based grid has nothing to do with liberal plots and everything to do with our own survival.

Out in the remote desert area of San Juan County known as the Valley of the Gods is the Valley of the Gods Bed and Breakfast, owned and operated by Gary and Claire Drogan. This B&B is interesting in several ways. It's built from a stone ranch house constructed by the grandsons of John D. Lee. The Lee family had an enormous influence on the history of southern Utah and northern Arizona, but that's not the point here (you can find out more about John D. Lee on the Internet). The truly interesting thing is what Gary Drogan has managed to do at the old Lee ranch. The four-room B&B and attached family quarters is run off-grid. Electricity is supplied entirely by a hybrid system of solar panels and wind turbines, with an emergency generator for backup. Water comes from a well, and a gray-water system ensures that little of the precious fluid goes to waste. The stone mass of the home's walls helps to maintain a comfortable temperature during brutally hot summers and harshly cold winters. Supplemental heating comes from a wood-burning stove and an indoor kitchen. There's an outdoor kitchen for use in summer to keep the house from heating up.

On the day I visited with the Drogans a chicken was cooking in a solar oven in front of the giant shade porch on the south side of the B&B. Behind a shed to the rear of the house is a processor for vegetable oil, which powers two of the three vehicles. What the Drogans have done is amazing not just because of the remoteness of their location, but equally because of what they've done in the face of the local political atmosphere. Gary is trying to get more people in the area involved in solar and wind projects, and he's helping local Navajo families to produce their own electricity in places it's never been before.

Some of the photos in this book come from the Drogans' B&B and other sites where open-minded, independent people have developed successful off-grid environments. With some luck these successes will inspire others to try to do the same, and with even more luck such successes could inspire a general change in attitude in our friends and neighbors who find it hard to believe that energy independence can be anything but evil or impossible.

Dave Black
Blanding, Utah
2008

Chicken cooking in a solar oven at the Valley of the Gods B&B.

CHAPTER 1
Living Off the Grid:
What It Is, What It Isn't

Defining "Off the Grid"

Put dozens of people of all ages in a room. Liberals and right-wingers. Wealthy, middle-class, and dirt poor. Athletes, soldiers, blue- and white-collar workers, criminals, priests . . . the entire range of American humanity. Ask them what "off-grid" means, and you'll get dozens of definitions that relate to unconventional people, things, trends, and actions.

To a teenager an off-gridder would be somebody who doesn't use social networking sites like MySpace or Facebook.

To a detective or researcher it could mean being untraceable, unrecognizable, and unrecordable through normal means.

To a paranoid, antisocial person or a criminal on the run, it might mean going underground and avoiding all recordable forms of commerce, using only cash in order to avoid any traceable transactions.

To an extreme sportsman it could mean doing cutting-edge, death-defying feats in exotic international locations.

To college science students, their genius but absentminded professor might be referred to as "off-the-grid."

For our purposes, I'll define *off-grid* as a state or degree of self-sufficiency with minimal reliance on public utilities, especially the three traditional basics: energy (power), water, and waste management. Sites that are truly off-grid provide their own energy, water, and waste management independent of public utility services.

REASONS TO GO OFF-GRID

- *There is no grid available.* This may be by choice or by fate. Many people in Third World countries and even in rural America do not have access to all the traditional grid utilities. It may be that you're rich and have found your dream property but it's too far out in the boondocks to tie into the grid. Or perhaps you're dirt poor and you're off-grid because you live in the squalor of a grid-less mud village high in the Andes. You might live in a religious community that shuns modern conveniences. For whatever reason, the traditional grid is absent.

- *To minimize the environmental impact of the grid.* To reduce your "carbon footprint" and allow the Earth to recover from everything we've done to it.

- *To avoid the high cost of traditional utility connections.* This reasoning belongs largely to the wealthy who have multiple properties that are only intermittently in use.

- *To save money by lowering utility bills.* This is a pipe dream under the current circumstances. You have to spend money to save money, and becoming self-sufficient costs a lot of money. For a huge investment you might make utility bills disappear, but you will still have monthly costs (battery replacement, etc.).

- *To ensure you have services when the grid goes down.* This is probably the best and most rational reason for minimizing your reliance on the grid. You may be a survivalist, or just average parents making sensible arrangements to take care of your family in a disaster.

- *To entertain an intelligent mind.* If you like to tinker with mechanical and electronic gadgets, and you actually like physics and chemistry and electronics, this is definitely the life for you.

- *To reduce our national dependence on fossil fuels, especially oil.* In 2007 and 2008 we all watched in disgust as oil prices dragged us into economic purgatory. Meanwhile, our kids were still getting shot and blown up on the streets of Baghdad in a "war on terror" that is more about oil than terrorism. Perhaps there's no revenge like economic revenge. We should work hard to be in a position to boycott oil from antagonist states instead of invading them.

- *Public image.* This is the worst reason for going off-grid. Being able to go green implies many things, among them wealth and political influence. It's like a mob boss going to church on Sunday.

The reasons range from altruistic to egotistic, from political to environmental, and from financial to geographical. Whatever the reason for going off-grid, there are some realities the budding off-gridder will be faced with.

First, unless you have the money to pay a contractor to turn your home into its own independent utility, you are going to have to make some changes to your lifestyle, learn a lot of technical stuff, and change your daily routine. This includes an intense concentration on energy conservation. You may also find that off-gridding changes your social routines, especially if you're moving from one location to another. How do you handle isolation? If you find yourself in a grid-tied community, will you be able to adapt to the cultural subtleties of the new community and its attitudes about green living?

Is it going to bother you to be the village oddball? On the other hand, if you find yourself in an off-grid community, will you be able to integrate with a bunch of people who you yourself might consider oddballs?

Second, you need money. If you're someone who will never own land or a home and who is completely dependent on other people for your lifestyle, you will never get off-grid. And the more extreme the climate you live in, the more it will cost you to go off-grid. That doesn't mean you can't do some small but very beneficial projects. For instance, a backup hybrid solar/generator system can be fun to build and relatively inexpensive, and it will give you emergency lights and run your TV and computer and refrigerator when the grid goes down. From another perspective, you can do a lot just by staying on the grid and learning to be an expert on energy conservation. In the end it will cost you less, save you more, and put less demand on the grid.

Third, you are never completely off-grid. You drive a car (with gas at nearly $5 per gallon) or ride a bike on a network (a grid) of roads that take you to and from work, school, church, market—all places that are run on the grid. All your off-grid gear is made at on-grid factories and transported by grid-dependent vehicles using fossil fuels. You may generate the electricity to power your TV and satellite receiver, but the programs you're receiving are coming through a grid. So is that wireless Internet. Ultimately, the money you use to buy your off-grid lifestyle comes from a grid-dependent career. Get over it. There is no life without a grid of some kind.

This book is for those who have a genuine interest in off-grid projects and who truly want to make a positive impact on their lives and the lives of the people they love. There's no hype here. No exaggeration. No product endorsements. No complicated do-it-yourself plans. No promises. Just plain, simple information and some suggestions on where to get more.

CHAPTER 2
Conservation

It's nice to be off-grid, but let's be honest—it changes your lifestyle. Before spending thousands of dollars to get off the grid, do a dress rehearsal. Do everything you're going to have to do to conserve energy while you're off-grid. This will help you in several ways: First, you might find that you can reduce your utility bills by so much that going off-grid is financially unreasonable. Second, you'll be able to judge more accurately what your absolute minimum needs will be when it comes to sizing your alternative power systems. Third, it proves that you're sincere about making a difference, rather than just projecting a pious image to dazzle your peers.

It's hard to talk about conservation without referring to buzzwords like *global warming*, *greenhouse gases*, and *carbon footprint*. Most Americans have no idea what a carbon footprint is, and in a few years there will certainly be another buzzword to replace it. But let's take a look at the concept. Your carbon footprint is the direct effect your actions and lifestyle have on the environment in terms of carbon dioxide emissions. An average American supposedly produces about 40,000 pounds of CO_2 emissions every year, and it's CO_2 that's largely to blame for the human contribution to global warming. So when I talk about these energy conservation steps, I'm not only giving you a way to downsize your utility bills and to rehearse for your off-grid lifestyle; I'm also giving you some practical suggestions on how to significantly reduce your carbon footprint. If you're building a new home, it's easy to simply just incorporate these recommendations into your building plans. If you're already in your permanent home, you'll find that retrofitting a home to meet these standards can be quite costly. Fortunately, most of the suggestions given here will provide a quick return in terms of reducing your utility bill.

Landscaping

Plant some shade trees in strategic locations around your home to keep it cooler in the summer. Keep shrubbery away from the vents of your air conditioner. Combine that with some *xeriscaping*—a method of landscaping that conserves water. These are the ideas behind it:

- Planning and design based on your regional climate and microclimate.

- Appropriate selection and zoning of plants that can flourish in those climates (often native species considered to be weeds by your water-hogging neighbors).

- Limiting grass or turf that requires heavy watering. In some cases you may need to let your lawn grass die, or kill it, to keep it from competing with your xeric plants.

- Soil improvement. Improved soil increases absorption and moisture retainment. Soils improved with organics also provide essential nutrients to plants. Tilling, grading, organics and other improvements should be done before the installation of watering systems.

- Adequate, efficient irrigation or watering. Determine how much your plants actually need, and take into consideration *evapotranspiration* (ET rate = the amount evaporated from the soil plus that transpired through the plant's leaves), and don't overwater them. Get the ET rate from your local extension service. When you water or irrigate, do so in the morning when the evaporation rates are low. If using sprinklers, use sprinklers that throw big drops. Small drops and mists are blown away or evaporate in the heat before they hit the ground. Many xeriscapers recommend gravel as a substitute for mulch because it collects dew.

- Use of compost and mulch to provide nutrients, slow evaporation, maintain improved soil, and retard weed growth.
- Adequate maintenance, including pest control, pruning, and weed control.

Energy-Efficient Appliances

When buying a new appliance, take the time to look at the yellow Energy Guide labels. These labels tell you the energy efficiency of the appliance, and will actually show you how much energy the appliance uses compared to similar models. This is shown in a white box in the center of the label and may start with the words THIS MODEL USES. . . Energy Guide labels are required by the Department of Energy (DOE) on new appliances that have a fairly wide range of energy efficiencies between models, including refrigerators, freezers, water heaters, dishwashers, clothes washers, air conditioners, heat pumps, and furnaces. Appliances having little difference in efficiency between models, such as kitchen ranges, clothes dryers, and microwave ovens, are not required to carry the label.

A second label you might see on new appliances is ENERGY STAR; this is an EPA voluntary labeling program designed to help shoppers identify more energy-efficient products with the goal of reducing greenhouse gas emissions from power plants. ENERGY STAR–labeled appliances exceed federal efficiency standards. An ENERGY STAR–qualified appliance also carries the Energy Guide label, and Energy Guide labels sometimes tell if the product is ENERGY STAR–qualified. Use these labels to comparison-shop. Highly efficient appliances are often more expensive, but over the lifetime of the appliance, you will more than make up the difference with the savings on your utility bill.

When you get a new appliance, think practically about all the bells and whistles; for instance, manual-defrost refrigerators use a third less energy than auto-defrosters.

Home Improvements

Add some insulation. If you're building a new home, exceed the local recommendation for insulating walls and ceilings. It will cut down on both heating and cooling bills. Also, insulate hot-water and hot-air ducts and pipes that provide heat around the house. Put a thermostat-controlled fan in the attic to exhaust hot air.

Replace ordinary single-glazed windows with argon-filled double-glazed or thermopane windows. Storm windows and doors significantly reduce heat loss. Covering the window frame inside with clear plastic does the same job, but be wary when the weather warms up: The temperatures between the glass and the plastic can cause the glass to crack if it's hit by cold rain, and can melt any plastic imprisoned between the two layers. Commercial reflective films can screen out heat without significantly reducing the light coming through, or the view out of the window. Add some exterior awnings over south-facing windows. Drapes and shades will buffer the home from heat and cold.

Paint your house an appropriate color. Dark shades are better in cold environments, as they collect more heat; light shades are best in warm climates, reflecting solar energy.

Weatherize your home with caulk and weather stripping to block air leaks around doors, windows, and cracks in the walls.

Lighting

Use screw-in fluorescent bulbs to replace old incandescent bulbs. They use a quarter of the electricity and last about ten times longer. If you insist on using incandescent bulbs, get the "energy saver" variety, which are filled with a halogen gas that makes them burn brighter on less electricity.

Keep your light fixtures clean for more light. Take advantage of reflected light by painting walls and ceilings with lighter colors. Clean bulbs and fixtures, and good reflected light, means you'll need fewer watts to create the same illumination levels.

Another good method of reducing the watts you use is to sit down and draw a map of the house to determine your lighting need in each area. For example, you may not need a lot of wattage in hallways; you don't need to light up the entire living room; but you might need extra watts in the cooking corner of your kitchen, or where you sit to read in the living room. This is called *task lighting*, and it means that while general areas can remain dim or unlit, specific task or safety-hazard areas should be brightly lit.

Fluorescent lights use extra electricity to start up, so it doesn't pay to turn them off unless you leave the room for longer than ten or fifteen minutes. But if you use incandescent lights, you should certainly turn them off whenever you leave the room.

Timers, photosensitive controls, and motion sensors can save you money, too. Set a timer to turn lights on at predetermined times. A photo control turns lights on when the sun goes down or dark clouds obscure the sun, and back on when the sun comes back out. Motion sensors turn lights on when they detect movement. Most often you'll see motion detectors used for security purposes, but they can also help you save on your electric bill. The light goes on only for a predetermined number of seconds, and then turns off. It beats leaving those outside security or entrance lights on all night. Motion sensors come as complete fixtures, screw-in add-ons, or adapters, and many of them are photosensitive or timed to turn off during the day.

Ambient Heating and Cooling

If you have a central heating system, check the filters and clean or change them before they get dirty. In cold months keep your thermostat at the lowest temperature you are comfortable with (say, 68 degrees F in the daytime and 60 degrees overnight). Open curtains and blinds on sun-facing windows, but at night keep blinds and curtains closed to keep the warmth inside. Place pans of water near radiator tops and warm vents, or run a room humidifier. Moist air makes you feel warmer than dry air.

Have an HVAC professional check your heating system every couple of years.

For various reasons you should be sure to use an air conditioner that's the proper size for the area you're cooling. Too large, and the unit will turn off and on frequently. Too small, and it will run all day, and probably all night because it didn't get the area to a comfortable temperature before bedtime.

Locate your air conditioner on the shaded side of the house. An air conditioner in direct sunlight will use more energy than one running in the shade. Closing the fresh-air intake on hot days will save some energy, as the precooled air indoors is recirculated. Close off rooms that don't need to be cooled. If you're going to be out all day, consider putting your AC on a timer so it's off all day but will cool your home just before you get home.

In hot months keep the thermostat set as high as you can comfortably stand it (say, 78 degrees). Fans can help, circulating air and allowing you to keep the thermostat somewhat higher, and sometimes eliminating the need to run the air conditioner. Even large ceiling fans use only a small fraction of the electricity required to run an air conditioner.

When it's hot, avoid doing anything that would increase the humidity, like cooking, showering, or washing clothes. Do those tasks in the early morning or late evening when it's cooler. Also, ovens and other heat-generating appliances should be used only in the early morning or late evening.

Check your AC filter monthly and replace or clean it if it's dirty. Keep the condenser coils and fins clean (see the owner's manual for instructions).

Refrigeration

Make sure the fridge or freezer door shuts tightly. If not, clean or replace the seal. Keep the condenser coils clean (they're in the back or bottom of the fridge), using a vacuum or brush. If it has an energy-saver switch, turn it on.

Keep the fridge and freezer out of hot rooms, out of the sun, and away from heating vents and heat-generating appliances, like ovens, dishwashers, and space heaters.

Keep the freezer compartment full, but don't block the fan that circulates the cold air. A full freezer takes less energy to keep things frozen. Fill empty space with water bottles. If the power ever goes out, they'll help keep the freezer cold, and you can transfer a few of them down to the refrigerator to keep it cold too.

Maintain the refrigerator temperature between 34 and 40 degrees F, and the freezer between 0 and 5. Any colder than that is a waste of energy. The only way to be absolutely sure is to have a thermometer in the compartment. They're cheap and available at any discount store.

Laundry

Wash heavily soiled clothes in warm water, and lightly soiled clothes in cold. Use detergents that are made to be effective in cold water. Rinse everything on cold. Warm or hot rinses don't make clothes cleaner. Wash full loads, not partial loads. If you're drying multiple loads, do them one right after the other. Don't let the dryer cool off between them. Don't overdry loads. It's expensive and it's not good for the fabrics. Dry heavy and light fabrics separately. If they're mixed, the total time the dryer runs will be longer. Clean the lint filter before every load. A clogged filter increases drying time. And remember the lost art of hanging clothes out to dry?

Hot Water

Turn your water heater thermostat down to 120 degrees. If your dishwasher doesn't have a temperature booster, set it at 130. If you're leaving the house for several days, lower the temperature until you get back. It's possible to set your electric heater on a timer so it heats only during the times you are most likely to need hot water, or so it turns off completely during the night.

Wrap your water heater in an insulating blanket or tape some fiberglass insulation around it. Some newer heaters are already insulated. As mentioned before, it's also a good idea to insulate hot-water pipes.

Repair leaky faucets as soon as possible. Use low-flow or flow-control showerheads in the shower.

Dishwashing

Rinse dishes with cold water before loading them, and start the dishwasher only with a full load. Consider allowing the dishes to air-dry.

Cooking

Use your microwave. It cooks faster and uses far less electricity than your electric oven.

When using your regular oven, it helps to cook several dishes at the same time and therefore at the same temperature. Don't open the door to see how things are going. Just opening the door will drop the temperature significantly.

Glass pans retain heat better than metal pans. With glass you can reduce preheating times and lower the temperature setting by 5 percent.

On the range-top, use pots and pans that have flat bottoms and that fit the burner. Cook with lids on the pans to shorten cooking time.

Transportation

Green and off-grid texts always devote a lot of space to alternative methods of transportation. The reason is that burning a gallon of gasoline supposedly produces 23 pounds of carbon dioxide. Although the math doesn't make a lot of sense (a gallon of gas only weighs 6 pounds), we get the idea. Not to mention that at the time of this writing, gasoline was more than $4 per gallon. Eventually, we simply won't be able to afford our gasoline-powered cars. The automakers are finally paying attention, and today, they are scrambling to develop electric and hybrid vehicles. Their success depends largely on the development of adequate battery technologies, emerging plug-in hybrid electric vehicles (PHEV) technology, and finding a place for biofuels such as ethanol, biodiesel, biogas, and hydrogen cell technologies. The eventual goal is to develop zero-emissions vehicles that do not burn fossil fuel, but are instead powered by alternative fuels such as hydrogen.

Hybrid and electric cars are still beyond the financial reach of most Americans. The people who need them the most are not going to be the people that get them . . . for now. In the meantime, here are some things the average person can do:

- Drive a vehicle that gets good mileage.
- Use a vehicle that can burn biodiesel or ethanol (although mechanics are finding some problems in vehicles that use ethanol).
- Use mass transit.
- Carpool.

CHAPTER 3
Leaving the Grid: Shelter

Land

It's interesting that regardless of their professed reasons for going off-grid, most off-gridders choose the land that their homes will sit on based on a simple factor: convenience. How close is the nearest Wal-Mart? The nearest hospital? The nearest school or university? People who profess to be off-gridders and yet make their decisions based primarily on such conveniences are, in a sense, still hopelessly attached to the grid.

The other factors off-gridders look for in their search for the perfect building site include:

- Good solar access, with south-facing slopes for passive heating and earth sheltering. Part of the land needs to have a good slope angle for backing the shelter into the slope (called "earth sheltering").

- Unobstructed access to the wind.
- Dry, well-drained land with stable soils, but land with a good water supply.
- Favorable climate for year-round comfort and microclimate, along with good topsoils conducive to growing food and providing shade and wind protection.
- On-site building resources (trees, rocks, sand, clay, etc.).
- No (or minimal) legal obstructions to off-grid development.
- Good views.
- No pollution.

The basic steps in putting your site together consist of finding the site, making a map of it, deciding on a house design and making detailed plans, and, finally, construction (or purchase) of the shelter.

There are, of course, millions of people who would like a break on their utility bills, and who can, with some help, turn what they already have into an off-grid home. Most people simply can't afford to run out and buy a piece of land, hire an architect and construction team to design and slap down an off-grid dream house, and live happily ever after. Let's be a little more realistic than that. We can start small by taking some conservation measures that will reduce our utility bills, and then work our way up from there.

Shelter requirements could be determined by distinguishing the basic venues available for off-grid living.

The first is the *transient venue*, consisting of lifestyles centered around mobile habitations (e.g., RVs), transient homes (tents, hogans, huts), and habitations that have less than a 250-square-foot footprint.

The second is the *intermittent venue*, which includes seasonally or permanently inhabited fixed or mobile habitations (cabins, larger motor homes, and trailers) that have a footprint between 250 and 750 square feet.

The third is the *permanent venue*, which includes fixed habitations with a footprint of more than 750 square feet. These are the homes of America's middle and upper economic classes.

Before we get into the details of shelter in the three venues, let's take time to examine passive solar design. A knowledge of the principles of passive solar design can be used to make inexpensive improvements even in homes that weren't designed to take advantage of solar energy.

Passive Solar Design

Passive solar design is a method of heating and lighting a space with the least input from the grid. Here are the major parts of the solar design puzzle:

COMPONENTS

- *South-facing windows.* These should allow low-angled winter sun to enter. The sunlight is converted into heat and stored in a thermal mass.
- *Thermal mass.* This is heat-absorbing material in walls (known as Trombe walls), floors, and ceilings, and includes brick, stone, concrete, drywall, tile, and earth materials. The function of thermal mass is to convert sunlight to heat, radiate that warmth, and store excess heat for later use (to keep you warm all night long).
- *Overhangs.* Overhangs regulate solar gain. As we all know, the angle of the sun relative to the earth changes. It's greatest in summer and lowest in winter. The overhangs (the eaves) control how much sun gets into the house by shading windows and walls from the high-angled summer sun. As the angle of the sun gets lower in winter, more sunlight gets inside, making more heat.
- *Insulation and window coverings.* These should form an uninterrupted layer through walls, ceiling, foundation, and over windows and skylights. This insulation layer will keep warmth inside during the winter, and heat outside during the summer.
- *Ventilation.* Necessary to spread the warm or cold air evenly.

How much heat can the sun make in the winter? These blinds, sandwiched between a glass window and a thin layer of plastic sheet, melted under the heat generated in that space by direct sunlight and the light reflected off the snow. The ambient temperature outside that afternoon was 24 degrees.

There are many ways of designing a home to take advantage of solar energy. The simplest designs are *sun-tempered*, a term that means the design takes advantage of the most obvious methods of collecting the sun's energy. For instance, solar heat collection will be maximized when the long axis of the house runs east-west; when there are many windows or a few very large windows along the south side; and when the house is well insulated, or may have thermal mass added.

A true solar design includes even more south-side window space, more insulation, and more thermal mass. This structure gets lots of direct heat gain from sunlight through the windows, which is retained by the thermal mass. Attached sunspaces can collect heat through their south-side windows and transfer that heat by convection—and with the help of small fans—through doors, windows, or vents into the house. This is referred to as *isolated-gain passive solar*. The true solar structure will have an effective thermal mass, often called a Trombe wall, made of earth, brick, or cement and often painted black.

Other factors come into play when trying to solarize a home. Basically the rule of thumb is to keep it simple and keep it small. Here are some important points to bear in mind:

FACTORS TO REMEMBER

- *Large structures are harder to heat than small structures.*

- *An east-west axis (90 degrees to true south) allows the longer side of the structure to be exposed to the sun.* That's where the big windows should be. North- and east-facing glass can lose a lot of heat in the winter, and west-facing glass can cause overheating in summer, so they should be few and small. (Use overhangs over the windows to protect the interior from too much summer sun. A 2-foot overhang is usually enough.)

  If possible, burrow into a south-facing slope and build the structure with its north side buried in the berm. This is called *earth sheltering.*

  Thermal mass inside collects heat in the winter and stays relatively cool in the summer, which helps prevent overheating. The thermal mass should be widely dispersed inside so it warms the whole structure. Narrow rectangular masses help heat multiple rooms independently without fans or ducts, and they help block the sun from the interior surface of the east and west walls.

- *Insulate the structure.* Exceed the insulation levels required by code. Protect insulation from moisture, as moisture decreases thermal resistance. It is especially harmful to cellulose and fiberglass insulation. Vapor barriers on walls may help some, but moisture usually attacks through penetrations like loose fittings around doors, windows, roofs, or through small holes in the walls. Be sure to comprehensively caulk and flash these penetrations.

Batt insulation should not be compressed and should be flush against framing. Liquid foam products make an airtight seal and repel water. Insulated windows are important on the east-, north-, and west-facing walls. Cover windows at night with insulated shades or rigid thermal shutters.

- *Consider radiant barriers on the roof.* Internal ventilation is important to spread the heat evenly.
- *Build structures that are as airtight as possible.* Seal penetrations to prevent infiltration of cold air and exfiltration of heat in the winter, and infiltration of warm air and exfiltration of cold air in the summer. A sealed entryway (sometimes called an *airlock*) prevents air from rushing in and out when the main structure's doorway is opened. Earth sheltering also reduces in- and exfiltration, and it reduces heat loss to exterior wall space and roofs. It also provides a thermal blanket around the structure that helps keep it warm in winter and cool in summer.

- *Keep some sun-free areas in the structure.* If it gets too hot, they'll provide some relief.
- *Maintain a source of backup heat, such as a propane heater, woodstove, or low-watt electric space heater.*

Transient Shelters

Let's not confuse this venue with the austerity of homelessness. We're not talking about sleeping in cardboard boxes or stowing away in a freight car. These are homes and other habitable structures, and there are more of them out there than you might think.

Tents and Soft Shelters

Tents have been used by nomadic people since well before recorded history. An example is the tepee, used by some Native American tribes. Even today many people, such as the Bedouins of the Arabian Peninsula, still live in traditional tents. Tents are the mainstay of modern armies behind the front lines. They serve as a key piece of gear for individuals and groups that venture into the backcountry for recreational or exploratory purposes. They are also used for emergency housing and storage during disasters. In moderate climates at low latitudes and where marine currents generate a consistently

Anasazi ruins in southeast Utah imply a good understanding of passive solar heating and cooling a thousand years ago.

comfortable environment, tents are a reasonable choice for independent living or vacationing on a tight budget.

Tents possess three major selling points: First, they're economical; second, they're portable; and third, they're quick and easy to set up.

Tents can be made from many different materials, but nylon and cotton canvas are the most commonly used. Nylon is the material of choice today due to its light weight and its inability to absorb significant moisture. Nylon materials are often coated with substances like silicon and polyurethane that make them almost

A thousand years later, a modern home in the same canyon uses the same principles.

completely waterproof. The disadvantage of nylon is its tendency to break down under UV radiation (i.e., sunlight). A seasonally inhabited tent may last a few seasons, but a permanent nylon habitation would be lucky to survive a year in the sunlight. Considering the cost of a tent compared to that of a "hard shelter," they're a better deal even if you have to replace them once a year. Cotton canvas is heavy and it absorbs water easily (making it even heavier). When it absorbs water, the threads swell and become so tightly packed that the tent eventually becomes temporarily very water-resistant.

Brochure and photo detailing the Zion National Park Visitors Center's passive solar design and structure.

Tents come in all shapes and sizes. Most of the popular tents on the market are dome tents that are supported by external poles. Some additional features that you'll want are poles and/or flies (rain covers) that are shock-corded to the main frame. Double-wall construction increases the weight, but also increases durability and weather-resistance. Bug-screened windows and doors are nice. Dual zippered doors and windows are another plus.

Since we're talking about zippers, be forewarned that the zippers on a cheap tent will be the first thing to go and can only rarely be repaired, leaving you with a tent that has doors and windows that won't close. If you're buying a cheap tent, as soon as you get it home, make sure you check the zippers and trim away any loose threads or material that can get caught in the zipper. The next things to fail on your cheap tent will be the stake loops and the fabric channels that attach the tent to the frame. These fail because the material is of poor quality and the sewing is weak. If you're buying a cheap tent, consider using your surge sewing machine to double- or triple-stitch any of the seams and channels that will be highly stressed. Stitching a patch to a weak point may also spread the stress over a wider area and prevent it from tearing.

So, just what is a "cheap tent"? Let's just say that if you're paying less than $1 a square foot for floor space, you're probably buying a short-lived lemon. This isn't always the case, but it's generally accurate. Buy brand names that you can trust.

Here are some additional factors to consider when choosing a tent home:

Living Area

You want plenty of room for yourself, your roommates, and your stuff. Sixty square feet of floor space per person is about the minimum you'll need to keep from getting claustrophobic. Add some area for a few other amenities (i.e., table and chairs), and if you want to be able to fit a few guests in on occasion, you'd better double the space (120 square feet minimum). Unless you're cooking outside or in a side tent, add another 40 square feet for your kitchen. We're up to 160 square feet.

Do they really make tents that size? Yes. Take the Eureka Copper Canyon 1610. This is a vertical-wall cabin-style tent with an 80-square-foot bedroom and an 80-square-foot screened-in room. The screens have roll-back storm covers, so the entire tent can be kept dry in a storm. It has an extension cord port and lots of loops to hang lights from. It also has a ceiling height of 7 feet. The ceiling height (head space) is important if you're actually going to turn a tent into a home. Not being able to stand up straight in your own home is a real letdown. The cost of this tent: $2 per square foot.

Is there anything bigger? Yes. Take, for another example, the Eureka Condo, which is a three-room, 10 1/2 x 20-foot cabin tent with great head space. It goes for about $3.80 per square foot.

Durability

You want a tent with hefty, strong poles that will not allow the tent to collapse or lay down in the wind or under the load of a moderate snowstorm. Seams should be double-sewn and sealed, and the windows and doors should have heavy-duty zippers. A *three-season tent* is designed for mild climates or for use in spring, summer, and fall. They perform well in windy conditions as long as the poles are sturdy and correctly attached, the tent is staked, all the guy lines are staked, and the fly and guy lines are tensioned correctly. Three-season tents have fewer poles, lighter materials, and less aerodynamic designs than what are called *four-season* or *expedition tents*. A good four-season tent is worth the extra expense.

Protection from Water

Many poorly made tents come without a rain fly, relying solely on their waterproof material to keep the rain out. Avoid these. Condensation from breathing and cooking will collect on waterproof ceilings and run onto the floor or onto the occupants. On the other hand, some expensive tents are made from breathable, vapor-barrier material and manage to shed rain and minimize condensation. To be on the safe side, get a tent with a rain fly. Tents that incorporate a rain fly are called "double-walled tents." The fly should cover most of the tent and certainly any windows or skylights that cannot be zippered shut. Look for a tent whose fly has tension adjustments and is shock-corded (the tie downs or stake loops are elasticized). A vestibule is a floorless extension of the tent. The sleeping area of the tent can be sealed off completely from the vestibule. This makes vestibules ideal for changing out of dirty clothes and shoes before going into the main tent.

Protection from Bugs

All openings, including vents, doors, and windows, should have bug screening. If you're in an area that has a continuous problem with particularly nasty invaders (like scorpions or centipedes), use duct tape to seal any holes that are not screened (e.g., the utility port).

There are many reliable tent manufacturers that make and sell tents of similar size and quality. Look at consumer reports on the Internet to get an idea of the tent's quality. Visit your local sporting goods store to actually see and touch the tent before you buy it.

Yurts

The word *yurt* is a westernized Asian word that refers to traditional round dwellings used by nomadic peoples. In North America and Europe, the word immediately brings to mind the modern variants. In Europe, this is usually a trellis-walled dwelling made of canvas. In North America it can refer to several wooden-framed round dwellings, such as *tapered-wall* and *frame-panel yurts*, or a portable round dwelling called the *fabric yurt*. In many cases the distinction between a tent or cabin tent and a yurt is minuscule.

Yurts use a collection of roof poles attached to a center ring. The far ends of the roof poles are embedded in a fortified top-of-the-wall perimeter, and as gravity pulls down the heavy center-ring joints, the roof poles are pushed outward into the perimeter, creating a ceiling that needs no internal supports such as posts or center poles. Only the walls need support, which is provided by circumferential trellis-like framing. The round shape and the steep roof provide wind resistance and effectively shed snow and rain.

So what's the difference between a yurt and a big tent, or a cabin tent? For one thing, yurts are usually placed on a wooden platform. Many other materials can be used as a foundation. Even cob has been used (a mixture of sand, clay, water, and straw). In desert or arid climates a yurt can be set directly on the ground. To improve drainage, a rock-filled trench can be constructed around the yurt foundation.

Two other things distinguish a yurt from a tent: the time it takes to construct it, and the cost. Yurts designed with high-tech materials will cost an average of more than $15,000, although it's quite possible to buy the plans and materials for a small yurt for as little as $3,000.

Tents are assembled in a matter of minutes. Even giant commercial event tents rarely take more than a few hours to set up. Yurts, on the other hand, typically take days to weeks. Yurts are simply far less portable than tents, in spite of their nomadic beginnings. In addition, building codes are not kind to yurts, tents, or any other structure that can be deemed "temporary" or "closed-quarters." Local governments and snobby neighbors often view them as unhealthy eyesores that represent a step backward. In most cases code compliance will require a at least flushing toilets and running water.

Traditional Native American Dwellings

A number of modernized versions of traditional Native American dwellings are commonly used, and some can be easily and inexpensively constructed.

The tepee is probably the best-known Native American dwelling. To erect a tepee, a cone-shaped frame of long wooden poles is set up. Three or four main poles are staked in the ground first, and fastened together near the top; then, other poles are added to form a roughly circular base. A waterproof cover, traditionally made from animal hides but now more often made from canvas, nylon, or even plastic, is pulled over the frame. A hole at the top permits smoke to escape from a central fire or stove. This opening is adjustable with outer flaps on the cover and can be closed in wet weather. Stones or stakes hold the bottom edges of the tepee cover in place, but in the heat of summer, the cover can be rolled up for ventilation. An inner lining of insulation is often added for cold climates. A 25-foot (in diameter) tepee kit can be as inexpensive as $1,500. One wonders why a commercial tepee costs so much less than a yurt when the two are so similar.

The hogan, the traditional Navajo (Diné) home, is a round or polygonal (six-sided or eight-sided) domed house made of logs or poles and plastered with mud or earth. The entrance traditionally faces east to greet the rising sun. It has one large room, up to 25 feet in

A traditional Navajo hogan, framed with timbers and covered with dirt.

diameter, designed for a single family. The Navajo tended to live in isolated groups of several related families, each of which had its own hogan. Hogans are still in use around the Four Corners of Colorado, New Mexico, Utah, and Arizona.

The Pueblo Indians lived in distinctive, apartment-like building complexes made of stone or adobe bricks (sun-baked clay and straw) and supported by wooden beams. Some of these dwellings, centuries old, are still in use today. The Southwest is peppered with the ruins of Anasazi and Fremont cultures, who used this type of construction effectively, with passive solar benefits, on the sides of cliffs and beneath rock overhangs to achieve comfortable communities in a harsh land.

Recreational Vehicles (RVs)

An RV, also known as a motor home (in spite of some arguments to the contrary), is an enclosed wheeled or motorized platform dually used as a vehicle and a dwelling. They offer more mobility and protection than a tent or a tepee, and buck for buck, about the same living space and comfort as a yurt. Unfortunately, there are a lot

Class A motor home.

of RVs out there that look nice but fall to pieces with any serious use. Check with consumer organizations and get an RV that's for living in, not merely for vacation traveling. Here are the categories of RVs or motor homes:

Class A Motor Home: A home built on a commercial bus, big truck, or specialized chassis.

Bus Conversion: A commercial bus converted to a motor home. Some of these get ridiculously fancy.

Class B Camper Van: This is essentially a conventional van with an added raised roof or a low-riding backside.

Class C motor home.

Pop-up tent or folding trailer.

Class C Motor Home: These are van- or truck-like compartments built on a truck chassis with an attached cab section. The cab-over profile is distinctive and contains a bed or an entertainment center. These are also known as mini motor homes.

Truck Camper: This is a compartment temporarily placed on the bed of a pickup truck. A camper has insulated walls, a small kitchen, a heater, and sometimes a small bathroom. A camper shell is a single walled compartment with no frills. Shells can often be nicely customized to fit the needs of the owner.

Left, travel trailer. Right, teardrop trailer.

Folding Trailer (aka, Pop-Up Tent or Tent Camper): These collapse into small packages that make towing easier for smaller vehicles.

Travel Trailer: These units are designed to be towed by larger vehicles with bumper or frame hitches.

Teardrop Trailer: These small, lightweight, somewhat aerodynamic trailers are designed to be towed by tiny cars, motorcycles, and even bicycles. They essentially contain nothing more than a bed and some passive ventilation.

Hybrid Trailer: These are a mixture of travel trailer and tent trailer. They may have roofs or top sections of walls that can be lowered over the bottom section, or pullout tent sections.

Fifth-Wheel Trailers: These are the RVs you curse under your breath in traffic on steep hills. They are designed to be towed by a pickup truck, and hopefully it will be a medium- to heavy-duty truck

Fifth-wheel trailer.

with some guts. A special fifth-wheel coupling hitch is required. There's usually a cab-over, containing an entertainment center, a stash of hunting rifles and beer, or a couple of repulsive youngsters making faces and flipping off passing motorists.

Park Model: These are also known as vacation or resort models, and are designed for trailer park camping only. They are not capable of off-grid living without some extensive modification.

Toy Hauler: These are motor homes, fifth-wheels, or travel trailers that are part living space, part garage or stable (for horses, ATVs, motorcycles, etc.).

Home-Crafted RVs: These are units improvised from cars, vans, school buses, boats, etc. With a little imagination, some nice dwellings can be put together from these vehicles.

RV Features

At a minimum your RV will contain a bed (or beds), a table, and food preparation and storage areas. Larger, more expensive units will also have their own bathroom, a refrigerator, and may include a living room and a master bedroom. They may also have a converter, which changes the AC current found at camp hookups to the DC power needed to run most of the on-board appliances. Fancier units will have satellite TV, satellite Internet, slide-out sections (some slide out on both sides of the unit to make an enormous living room), and awnings. These road-hogs are usually big enough that they can also tow a small vehicle or a trailer loaded with ATVs.

RV Prices

New RVs can run from as little as $12,000 to as much as $2 million; $80,000 will buy a very large, practical, livable arrangement. (There are many for sale in my area for prices as low as $6,000.) Anything more than this is impractical, and the money would be better spent greening the mansion that the owners live in when they're not "roughing it."

RVs are great, especially if you actually have an off-grid RV unit. But let's face it: The majority of RVers are upper-middle-class kids looking for cushy digs in their cosmic quests for whatever, and the rest of them are retired people who just don't give two cents about green living in comparison to personal comfort and ease. Don't disrespect your own intelligence by thinking that staying at an RV park or an improved campground with all the amenities and full hookups is living off the grid. It's not even close. *Boondocking* is an RVer's term that means total off-grid living. Because of their high profile, it's hard for boondockers to find someplace to stay for any length of time without being accused of squatting. In the West, the Bureau of Land Management offers camping at no cost in most places, and although there could be limits on the number of days you can stay at a single site, another site is usually just down the road.

Powering RV Utilities

The "house batteries" of most RVs consist of a 12-volt system in parallel circuits to maintain voltage but to increase amperage. The batteries are kept separate and isolated from the interior of the vehicle, and are isolated from the vehicle battery. Batteries are rated in amp hours: amp hours x volts = watt-hours (the measure of how long a load can be run). Many RVs that use photovoltaic (PV) systems go with 24 x 36-inch panels that produce 100 to 120 watts. Since most RVs have both 12-volt and 120-volt systems, the inverters in an RV are likely to be rated to 1,500 to 2,000 watts. Unless the house batteries are beefed up or the solar array is enlarged, the performance of the 120-volt system may fall short of your needs.

The 12-volt system in the RV has its own fuses (usually automotive), receptacles, wiring, and power sources. Fuses are usually located behind a metal panel near where the power cord enters the RV. The correct size and rating is indicated by the color of the fuse and the number printed on it.

Using more than 50 percent of the battery capacity can permanently damage the RV batteries. Remember that these batteries usually supply the power for:

- lights
- thermostats
- kitchen fan
- slide-out motor
- stereo CD player
- lp gas detector

- water pump
- furnace fan
- bathroom fan
- refrigerator
- 12-volt TV
- inverter

Houseboats

Off-grid books avoid talking about houseboats as though they were carriers of the plague. In actuality, the difference between a houseboat and an RV is nothing more than a set of wheels.

A houseboat is a boat designed or modified to be used primarily as a home or dwelling. Houseboats are typically moored (fixed) or motorized and mobile. Mooring costs big money, and of course comes with varying hookup resources. Again, a fully hooked-up, moored houseboat is *not* off-grid. Also, marina costs can be hefty—$1,000 to $5,000 per year. In many areas of the world, including the United States, it's possible to live in a boat and never dock in the same place. Lake Powell, for instance, which extends into Arizona and Utah, has over 2,000 miles of shoreline pitted with deep inlets, unspeakably beautiful scenery, great fishing, and a pleasant climate. It's often called America's favorite houseboating destination.

Houseboats usually range from 30 to 70 feet in length and can supply as much as 2,000 square feet of living space. A small family could easily get along with a 40-foot boat. Houseboats are stocked with the same amenities as RVs, and are actually comparable in price. There are now houseboats on the market that are factory wired with hybrid electricity generating systems that can supply lots of power without burning propane or gasoline.

Occasionally someone will use a yacht as a house-boat, but livable yachts are even more expensive than houseboats.

There are definite advantages to buying a new boat. First, the warranties are in place, and the accessories and systems should all work flawlessly. Even so, incredible deals can be had by those willing to risk purchasing a used boat. A quick look on the Internet will deluge you with boats less than 35 years old that average $125 per linear foot. A lot of repair and modification can be done with the money you save. By the way, houseboats are often sold time-shared like condos (although these "condo boats" are usually heavily grid-dependent).

Manufactured Homes and Sheds

The term *mobile home* is used less often these days in deference to more graceful terms such as prefabricated, modular, and manufactured homes. Actually, these all fall under the general category of manufactured homes.

A manufactured home is a house that is constructed in a factory, and which meets federal guidelines and safety standards (HUD Code). They can include modular homes that are transported to the site in pieces and then assembled on-site; panelized homes, constructed in panels (e.g., wall and roof), and then transported and pieced together on-site; pre-cuts, which are essentially kits transported to and assembled on-site; and mobile homes, which are constructed entirely in the factory and then transported to the site.

These homes go for between $18,000 to $180,000. A single-wide dwelling with 600 to 800 square feet of floor space can cost as little as $21,000. A nice double-wide might cost twice that. Check the used and repo market too. The cost, of course, doesn't include the land it will sit on, but the savings you realize could be enough to convert the house to a substantial dwelling that could take you completely off the grid.

For those on a tiny budget or with more transient plans, a prebuilt shed might be just what you're looking for. Sheds come in any stage imaginable, from total preconstruction to kits, in steel, vinyl, wood, and plastic, and are usually placed on a pre-cut wooden floor or a concrete foundation. Between $1,000 to $4,000 will set you up in a shed with at least 288 square feet of living space. Take the money you save by not buying that mobile home and finish the shed with double walls, insulation, running water and a kitchenette, a toilet, a photovoltaic system, and some adequate ventilation. The big concern folks have about sheds is the offgassing from construction products used in building the shed. Sorry to upset your karmic buzz, but any new construction produces potentially harmful fumes. Your church. Your local bar and grill. Grandma's new apartment. Whatever.

Going for Broke: Manufactured Green Home

In 2007 a West Coast company introduced a fully manufactured green home that *Science Digest* described as "subtle, chic, and the epitome of modern-day sustainable living." You order the home and soon a load of green technologies and materials arrive and are assembled at your site. The concept is great. The home features water recirculation, a real toilet, energy-efficient foam insulation, LED lighting, a grass- and flower-growing roof, and rainwater storage for landscape irrigation.

The 1.5 kilowatt PV system lets you plug in your hybrid car and still have plenty of juice to power all your appliances. Every piece of the house has been planned to be eco-friendly. Sounds great, right? Here's the kicker: It's a one-bedroom, 700-square-foot dwelling that costs nearly $250,000, not including the land, the site preparation, or the installation. Um . . . excuse the pessimism, but low- and middle-class America is not ready for this. A converted mobile home would cost far less than half as much. As *Science Digest* implied, living green is easy, but not cheap.

Building Green on Your Own

With some capital and some time, a dedicated person can build a very comfortable green dwelling on his or her own. This is not meant to be a treatise on architecture and building materials. What I'm trying to do is give you some ideas. There are other sources that can talk you through the processes for each of these construction methods.

Log

Okay, we all want wood. It's chic, and a log home makes everybody think of you as the Daniel Boone of the modern world. But don't be fooled. Stick-frame, timber-frame, post-and-beam houses require heavy lifting, special tools, and a personal ability to justify the use of huge masses of wood.

Log homes need a solid foundation that will lift the logs off the ground. Logs are de-barked and joined by interlocking corner notches, with spaces filled with chinking (cement, mud, etc.). Chinking is prone to cracking and needs frequent repairs. In chink-less construction, logs are notched lengthwise and the notch placed onto the log below to make a tight fit.

Cordwood

Construction consists of mortar (cement or lime sand) placed on a concrete foundation in two parallel lines about 6 inches apart. Cordwood is placed directly on the mortar lines, perpendicular to and spanning them. The cordwood can be either round or split, and is worked into the mortar to create a strong bond. Insulation (sawdust mixed with lime for protection from insects and moisture) is placed in the spaces between the mortar joints, and the process is repeated. The wall will have good thermal mass and insulation.

Straw

When considering straw constructions, remember the difference between straw and hay. Hay attracts rodents because it's edible. Straw, on the other hand, has no nutrient value. Also, hay is more susceptible to composting.

Usually stacked-bale post-and-beam framing (the "fill-in method") or no framing at all is used. Bales from walls support the roof and upper stories, if any. This is called "load-bearing" straw-bale construction.

Plastered straw-bale walls hold up well against fire. To be durable, bale structures must have good roofs with adequate overhang and solid foundations that prevent moisture from seeping into the wall.

Adobe

Adobe consists of bricks fashioned from local subsoils and contains a mixture of clay, sand, and chopped straw or raw horse manure for strength. It is wetted, mixed, and poured into wooden forms and left to bake in the sun. After some drying the forms are removed and blocks are left to dry completely. Forms are reused.

For the walls, adobe bricks are laid in a running bond (overlapping pattern), just like modern bricks or stones, directly on a foundation. A mortar made of the same subsoil is used to hold the bricks in place. Earthen plasters are better suited for adobe than cement because they expand and contract at the same rate as the adobe bricks. This decreases cracking and repairs, and allows wall moisture to escape.

Adobe provides good thermal mass. Add insulation inside or outside for additional comfort.

Rammed Earth

This is a mixture of clay and sand compacted into forms. Sometimes cement is added to the mix. Wooden or steel forms are erected on the foundation. A 70 percent/30 percent mixture of moistened sand and clay is shoveled into the forms about half a foot at a time, and then tamped by a pneumatic compressor. When filled, the forms are removed. The block is usually 12 to 18 inches thick and 6 to 8 feet long. A new form is placed next to it. The walls, then the roof, windows, and door frames are built in order.

The advantages of rammed-earth construction are fireproof walls with good thermal mass. The disadvantages include the numerous forms and heavy equipment required to make and move the blocks.

Rammed-earth tires are a variation of basic rammed-earth construction. These dwellings are typically built into south-facing slopes. Tires are laid out on compacted soil, in a U-shape for one room. Cardboard is placed under the tire to prevent the dirt filling from leaking out. One worker fills the tire while the other tamps it. After the first row is completed, a second row is placed on the previous row in an overlapping (running) pattern, and the process continues until the wall is finished. A roof is attached. The walls are mud-plastered or finished with cement stucco.

The disadvantage of these rammed-earth tire "earthships" (as they're sometimes called) is that they can be damp. Protect the walls and foundation from ground moisture. Waterproof the walls, and install a French drain (a ditch filled with gravel and rock that redirects surface- and groundwater away from the structure).

Cob

Cob is a mixture of sand, clay, water, and straw, applied directly to the foundation by hand or shovel, and then massaged into shape. Most of the work is done by hand or by simple hand tools. Walls are whitewashed, lime-plastered, or coated with earthen plaster to protect them from rain. Add insulation in cold climates. In rainy climates, protect the walls with large overhangs or durable plasters or both (lime/sand plasters are good).

Earthbags

This method uses the same polypropylene bags that are used to store and ship grain. Fill the bags with a slightly moistened mixture of sand and clay. Lay them flat on the foundation one by one and tamp each course to flatten and compress the "bricks." Add two strands of four-point barbed wire on top of each course to give tensile strength and to help secure the layers together. Lay the next course on top in a running pattern. Hand-tamp the new course and repeat.

Completed walls are plastered. Earthen or lime/sand plasters are preferred and adhere well without preparation. Earthbags provide excellent thermal mass but very little insulation.

Readers will notice that a lot of the construction methods mentioned above involve tamping to consolidate the sediment. If a pneumatic tamper isn't available, a makeshift tamper can be as easy as stomping with booted feet. Primitive tampers can be made by screwing

Rondoval yard: A traditional rondoval (round house) in Lesotho. These homes are made with stone and thatch, and the interior walls are plastered with mud that is rubbed with cow manure to produce a smooth finish.

a 12-inch-square piece of 1-inch plywood to the end of a 4 x 4 timber, or by drilling a hole into a stump or an 8 x 8-inch hardwood block and driving a 5-foot pipe into it.

Cast Earth

This type of construction is a proprietary process using a slurry of water, soil, and 10 to 15 percent heated calcium, poured into forms on a concrete foundation. The walls are plastered or finished with stucco for protection and cosmetic appearance. See the inventor's website at castearth.com.

Straw-Clay

This material is made from straw and a little clay slip (clay and water used as a binder). Slip is poured into the straw and mixed in until the straw surfaces are slightly wet. The mix is packed into 2-foot-high wooden forms attached to wall framing with lumber or posts. The mixture is then tamped by hand.

Bamboo reinforcing is installed by hand, for lateral stability, through holes drilled in framing members along the height of the wall. When a form is filled, a new one is added. After two are filled, the lower is removed for drying. When walls have dried, they are coated with plaster.

Straw-clay structures are fireproof, soundproof, and well insulated. Their disadvantage is that they dry very slowly.

Papercrete

This is a mixture of newspaper, sand, cement, and water. Paper is cut into small pieces and soaked for 24 to 48 hours, and then sand, cement, and water are added. Stir to a thick gray slurry that can be poured into block forms (like adobe forms) or directly into wall forms.

It slowly dries and sets up into solid blocks with good thermal mass and good insulation.

Set the blocks on the foundation in a running band pattern, mortared into place with wet papercrete slurry, and then plaster the exterior and interior surfaces. Fiber adobe is a variation that uses clay instead of cement as the binder. It dries slower, but is cheaper.

Stone

Stone must be laid on very sturdy foundations of stone or concrete, in a running bond pattern with cement mortar. The mortar holds the stacked stones in place and decreases air infiltration. Thick, uninsulated exterior stone walls work best in hot, arid climates. In cold climates, walls must be insulated.

Disadvantages of working with stone include its weight, and the fact that the work is slow and boring. In seismic areas, steel reinforcement is required due to stone's low tensile strength. Also, stone is cold, and moisture often condenses on interior walls. Eliminating the problem requires double-wall construction or interior wall insulation.

Slip-form stone buildings are built using slip forms — wooden forms placed squared and plumbed on a foundation. Selected stones are placed on the outer face of the form, one course at a time. Concrete is then poured into the form after each course to fill remaining space.

Insulated Concrete Forms (ICFs)

ICFs are hollow blocks of varying length made of rigid foam insulation (beadboard—aka, expanded polysty-rene). Used to build foundations and interior walls, they snap into place. When concrete is poured into them, manufacturers install plastic or steel cross-bridges that attach one side of the form to the other. The ICFs are left in place, and the foam sandwich produces a foundation or external wall with an R-35 insulation rating. See the glossary for an explanation of R-ratings.

The advantages of ICFs are their light weight, ease of handling and cutting, good seismic performance, and insect and fire resistance.

Hybrid Dwellings

Most natural-material builders use more than one type of building material. Many times unusual materials are used to build unusual spaces, to fill nooks and crannies, or to make fireplaces, bookcases, or other specialty components.

*   *   *

At this point let's assume that you have a shelter. The next three chapters will give you some suggestions on how to light it, water it, and manage its waste.

CHAPTER 4
Leaving the Grid: Energy

The ABCs of Energy

Unless you're a physicist or an electronics technician, in order to get through the next two chapters we're going to have to review all that stuff they tried to teach us in high school science class. This is the stuff that had us all saying, "Why in the world are they making us learn this crap? We'll never use this junk in our real lives." Well, surprise! Here it is, leering back at us like a smug mother-in-law.

Energy is needed in order for anything to happen, and when something happens, energy is converted from one form to another. Different forms of energy make different things happen. Energy comes in many flavors: electrical, heat, light, sound, solar, chemical, kinetic, and potential, to name a few. Chemical energy is energy that is released during chemical reactions. Food, like that breakfast you ate this morning, and fuels like

Plants use solar energy to create a bank of chemical energy that we refer to as "food."

coal, gas, and oil are storages of chemical energy. So are batteries.

Kinetic energy is the energy of movement. The faster an object moves, the more kinetic energy it has, and the slower it moves, the less kinetic energy it has. When moving objects hit stationary objects, some of the kinetic energy is transferred to the stationary objects, making them move.

Potential energy is the energy objects have due to their position in a force field, such as an electrical field, gravity, or magnetism.

Shooting pool is a good example of how kinetic energy is transferred from one object to another.

The Law of Conservation of Energy states that energy cannot be created or destroyed, but can change its form. As mentioned earlier, when something happens and energy is used, it is converted into a different form. The final forms in most energy conversions are heat and light. Even these final forms are not destroyed, but are so spread out into the environment that they become difficult to use. The *energy chain* of a flashlight is an example. Chemical energy in the batteries is changed to electrical energy. Electrical energy is changed to heat and light from the bulb, which is dispersed.

While much of our immediate energy needs are obtained by burning fuels, nearly all energy on earth comes directly or indirectly from the sun. *Solar energy* reaches the Earth in the form of electromagnetic energy, a form of energy that can travel across space. The sun warms the planet. Plants use energy from the sun to make their food, and therefore ours. And the sun's energy can be used to generate electricity using a solar cell, or to heat water using a solar collector.

Non-renewable energy sources are those that can only be used once to produce energy. They include fuels like wood, coal, natural gas, oil, etc. Sources of energy that are not used up (that is, can be produced faster than we can use them, such as sunshine, wind, and moving water, or that can be reproduced as needed) are called *renewable* sources.

Of the energy consumed by mankind, over 90% of it comes from the burning of fossil fuels—fuels formed from fossilized plant and animal remains—and wood. The remainder is just about evenly split between nuclear energy and energy from renewable resources.

The burning of fossil fuels results in the release of significant amounts of carbon dioxide (CO_2) and other gasses. Even so, to this day there are rational people who deny that the greenhouse effect, global warming, and acid rain can be partially blamed on the intense use of fuels.

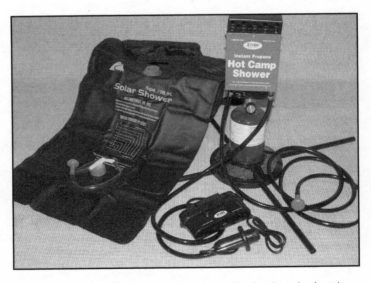

From left, a simplified solar water heater, the backpacker's solar shower, and a propane-heated camping shower.

Biogas is an interesting renewable fuel. Rotting organic matter produces methane, which can be used for space and water heating. It has also been used to power some automobiles and even jet aircraft. Among its negatives is the fact that although it's renewable, biogas is still a burned fuel.

In addition to solar energy, mentioned above, other renewable energy resources include wind and water. In a hydroelectric plant, moving water turns turbines that generate electricity. A wind farm generates

A solar water heater ("collector panel"). Radiated electromagnetic energy from the sun is absorbed by a black absorber panel, which heats the water in pipes connected to the panel.

electricity when the wind spins propellers that turn turbines.

In the scientific world energy is measured in joules (J). Power is the energy used over a specified period of time, and is measured in watts (W). One watt is equal to one joule per second.

Appliances and machines operate by taking one form of energy and changing it into another. An appliance is considered efficient if most of the energy used to operate it is changed into the energy that is needed. Fluorescent tube lights, for example, are more efficient

Wind turbine. The propeller is turned to face the wind. As it spins, it turns the generator of the turbine to create electricity.

A solar panel with individual cells visible. The cells convert the sun's energy into electricity when sunlight falls on a special layer of silicon and makes electrons move, creating a potential difference between layers. In this picture, lying below the solar panel array are a couple of old solar collectors.

than standard lightbulbs because they change more energy (electricity) into light and less into heat.

Heat 101

When a substance absorbs heat, its internal energy increases. Internal energy is the kinetic energy plus the potential energy of the atoms the substance is made of.

Heat flows from warm objects to cold objects, changing the internal energy of both. It continues to flow until both objects are at the same temperature. The objects that lose heat also lose internal energy. The objects that gain heat, gain internal energy.

Heat flow (or heat transfer) can occur by conduction, convection, or radiation.

In *conduction*, heat is transferred by molecular excitation within a material without any motion of the object itself. Energy is transferred as the excited particles collide with slower particles and transfer their energy to them.

In *convection*, heat is transferred by the motion of a fluid or gas. Heated gas or fluid expands and becomes less dense, becoming more buoyant than the gas or fluid surrounding it. It rises, moving away from the source of heat and carrying energy with it. Cooler gas or fluid sinks, and a circuit of circulation called a convection current is formed.

Radiation occurs when heat is transferred by electromagnetic waves that carry energy away from the source.

It takes 4,200 joules to raise the temperature of one kilogram (2.2 pounds) of water by 1 degree Celsius (1.8 degrees Fahrenheit). But some materials absorb heat better than others. Equal amounts of different materials require different amounts of heat to reach the same temperature. For example, it takes more heat energy to heat a quart of water to 100 degrees than it takes to heat a quart of oil to the same temperature.

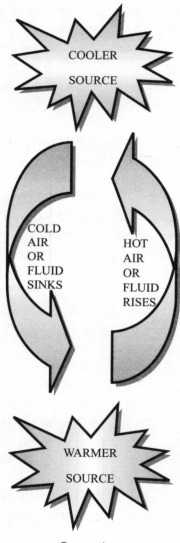

Convection

Temperature is a measure of how hot a material is. Materials have different specific heat properties (thermal capacities). Two equal masses of different materials—for instance, a quart of oil and a liter of water—will reach different temperature when heated with the same amount of energy. The oil will actually be hotter than the water. It's the difference in heat capacity that causes land masses to heat up faster than bodies of water, leading to sea breezes. Air warmed by the more rapidly heated land mass rises, and cooler air blows in from the body of water. These concepts of thermal capacity and heat transfer are important to understand when trying to design heat-efficient structures.

Temperature can be measured in several different scales. The scales most commonly used by those of us who are not scientists are the Fahrenheit scale (F) and the Celsius scale (C). The steam point and the ice point (the points at which steam or ice are produced) are the reference points on these scales. The ice point is 32 degrees F and 0 degrees C. The steam point is 212 degrees F and 100 degrees C. A degree of Fahrenheit is equal to $9/5$ Celsius plus 32. For most of the world, Celsius is easier to use than Fahrenheit because one degree represents 1/100th of the difference between the steam and ice points.

The Shocking Truth about Electricity

Remember what that science teacher tried to tell you back in high school about how the nuclei (specifically, the protons) of atoms are positively charged and the electrons around it are negative? Normally an atom has the same number of electrons as it does protons, so the atom is neutrally charged. But if an atom loses electrons to other atoms, it becomes positively charged, while the atoms that gain an electron have a negative charge. Electricity is a stream of negatively charged particles (electrons) flowing at the speed of light through a wire, similar to the way water flows through a pipe. Electrical forces exist between the charged objects, and the opposite charges "attract" (which simply means electrons want to flow *from* the negatively charged object *to* the positively charged object in order to get the objects back to their neutrally charged states). Substances through which a current of electrons can flow are called *conductors*. Substances through which an electron current cannot easily flow are called *nonconductors* or *insulators*.

In conductors—for example, metal wires—the electrons are free to move, and their movement is called the *current*. The path the current takes from one location to another—again, for example, the wires—is called the *circuit*. A circuit is a continuous pathway between a power source and an appliance or device (commonly referred to as "the load"). If the circuit is interrupted by an open switch or a blown fuse, the current stops. This electricity is converted to other forms of energy by the appliance or device, such as heat, light, or sound.

So, electrical current is a flow of electrons from an area of high electric potential (too many electrons) to an area of low electric potential (not enough electrons). It's this difference that makes the electricity flow, sort of like the flow of water from high pressure to low pressure. The potential difference is basically electrical pressure, and is measured in volts (V).

You will often hear the terms *alternating current* (AC) and *direct current* (DC). DC is the flow of electricity in one direction. AC, on the other hand, intermittently reverses direction because of the way it's generated. Batteries and PV cells produce DC because the current always flows from a fixed negative point to a fixed positive point. AC comes from generators whose poles change 60 times per second, causing the current to reverse directions. It's the type of current that enters your home from the utility grid. DC can be converted to AC by passing it through an inverter. Inverters are available with high AC power outputs and with conversion efficiencies of 90 percent.

The amount of current flowing through a circuit depends on the strength of the potential difference (volts) and the resistance of the components in the circuit. Current is measured in *amperes*. All materials, even conductors, resist the current to a certain extent, reducing the amount of current that flows. The *ohm* is the unit of measure for resistance. An ampere ("amp") is the current that will flow through one ohm of resistance with a "pressure" of one volt.

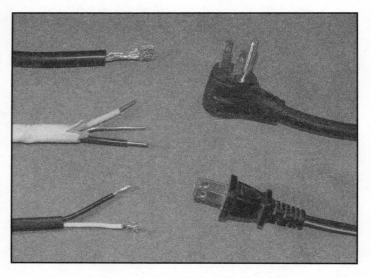

Left, a close-up of electrical cable and wire, made of a conductor (copper wire) and covered with an insulator (plastic). At right, plugs. Some appliances use a 2-pin plug and receptacle or socket. Others use a 3-pin plug. When a plug is put into a socket the pins connect with the hot (live) wires and neutral wires of the circuit. On most 2-pin plugs one prong is wider than the other. This keeps you from plugging the cord in incorrectly and reversing the polarity (the positive and negative parts of the circuit).

Components (such as lightbulbs) in an electrical circuit convert electrical energy carried by current into other forms of energy (heat and light). The components in a circuit can be arranged in two ways: series or parallel.

So what happens to voltages and current when they are stacked up in a series like the stack of batteries

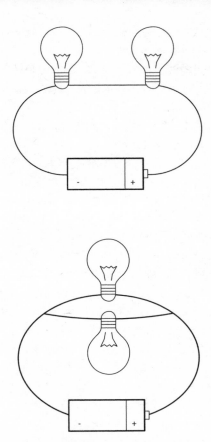

Top, a series circuit. The current flows through the components one after another. If one component stops working and breaks the circuit, no current flows. It's why an entire string of cheap Christmas lights stops working when a single bulb burns out. Bottom, a parallel circuit has more than one path for the current. If a component in one path stops working and breaks the circuit, current continues to flow through the other path.

in a flashlight? In *series*, voltages add up, but the amps (current) don't. In *parallel*, the amps (current) add up, but the voltage doesn't. Don't worry; I'll explain this again later when we look at how battery banks and solar panels are wired.

The amount of power (P) delivered by a given current (I) in amps, under pressure, or volts (E), is measured in watts. The formula is *power equals voltage times amps*, or P = EI. As you can see, watts (P), volts (E), amps (I), and ohms (R) are all interrelated and must be dealt with mathematically in order to understand electrical circuits and electrical systems.

Let's talk about watts in a little more detail. A watt is the amount of energy used per second and should be thought of as the rate of speed that energy is being used. The watt rating of an appliance is the rate or speed at which the appliance is using energy. For example, a 100-watt lightbulb uses 100 watts per second.

The unit of measure for electricity consumption is the kilowatt-hour (kWh). Check it out on your next power bill. Kilowatt-hours are the amount of energy used, and are figured by multiplying the rate of usage in kilowatts by the time in hours that the device runs. Don't let this term confuse you about how much power your appliance uses. Again, wattage is a rate; kilowatt-hours are the amount used.

A battery is a storage unit of chemical energy that is converted to electrical energy. The batteries familiar to

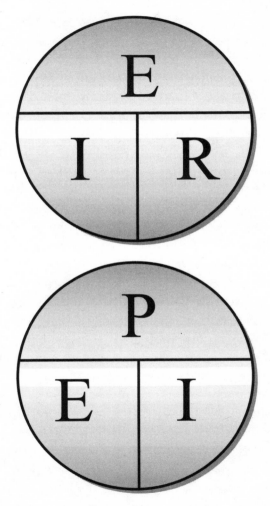

Use the circles to help remember the formulas for Ohm's Law
(I = E/R, E = IR, R = E/I) and for power (E = P/I, P = EI, I = E/P).

most people are the AAA, AA, C, and D batteries in their portable appliances and flashlights. These are called dry cells, and contain an electrolyte paste. An electrolyte is a substance that conducts electric current when used in a solution or paste. Chemical reactions make the charges separate and migrate to the appropriate terminal (positive or negative). When the necessary chemical properties of the electrolyte are depleted (when the battery "runs out of juice"), the battery is dead. Accumulators are batteries that can be recharged, like a car battery or like rechargeable flashlight batteries. Car batteries have a dilute sulfuric acid as the electrolyte that facilitates the potential difference between electrodes made of zinc and zinc oxide.

Household electricity is 110V (actually 110, 120, or 125V) or 240V, depending on what country you live in. Parallel circuits carry the electricity around the house. Appliances are often protected by fuses. The thin wire in a fuse melts under excessive current and breaks the circuit, stopping the flow of electricity.

Each parallel circuit in modern buildings contains three wires called the live ("hot"), neutral, and ground (or "earth") wires. The current is supplied by the live wires (usually black), and the neutral wires (usually white) carry the current back. The ground wire (usually green or bare copper) is a safety device that provides a path to the ground (earth) through which current can escape if the neutral wire is somehow broken or interrupted.

The electricity would otherwise take the shortest path to the ground—which could be you.

A current flowing through a wire produces a magnetic field. A wire wrapped around an iron bar behaves like a bar magnet when current is passed through it. The wire and bar are called an electromagnet. And if moving current can produce electromagnetism, it stands to reason that moving magnetism could produce electric current. And so it can. A generator is a machine that converts the energy of magnetic movement into electricity.

In a power station, electricity is created by turbines spun by steam or by moving water. The turbines then spin the shaft of a generator that has coils of wire (the armature) turning between two magnets. Turning the coil between two magnets induces a current that changes direction every half-turn. This is called alternating current, or AC. The amount of voltage generated depends on the number of turns in the coil, the strength of the magnetic field, and the speed at which the coil or magnetic field rotates.

In smaller systems (micro-hydro or small wind systems) we sometimes see the terms *AC generator* (also called an alternator) and *DC generator*. DC generators use a bridge rectifier to convert AC to DC to serve the battery banks. A rectifier is the opposite of an inverter. It changes AC to DC in a process called rectification. Rectifiers and inverters are known collectively as power supplies. A *power supply* is a device that converts one form of electricity to another and distributes it to the rest of the system.

Although most ample AC sources can be used directly if properly governed by devices, with the excess diverted to other useful purposes, many systems are dependent on storage batteries that require DC input. A properly governed AC generator can supply DC through a rectifier. But AC generator systems are commonly more expensive and complicated to set up than DC-generating systems.

Electronics is the use of devices or components to control how electricity flows through a circuit. Components include anything within the circuit that alters the path or intensity of the electrical energy: resistors, LED lamps, diodes, speakers, capacitors, antennas, and transistors.

Resistance is the ability of a material to resist the flow of electric current. All parts of a circuit have some resistance, which reduces the amount of current that flows around the circuit. When a material resists electric current, it converts some of that energy into heat and light. Resistance is measured in units called *ohms*.

Getting Wired

For most people, this is the confusing part, and it's where most do-it-yourselfers get screwed up.

In a common household circuit, 120V AC flows from a hot bus bar in a main service panel through a hot wire to a fixed appliance such as a lightbulb or to a component like a power socket. From there a neutral wire completes the circuit path back to the panel's neutral bar, which is grounded. If a circuit malfunctions, the ground wire provides a safe path to the power source for abnormal current flow. The grounding wire keeps you and any metal surfaces containing appliances—such as your computer housing—from becoming the path of abnormal current flow. It also enables overcurrent-protection devices such as circuit breakers to work.

Most people move into houses that have been wired by electricians and construction experts. A few of us do it ourselves, and we take the risks. This book is not meant to coach you through the wiring of a home or building with local utility power as the main power source. Hire an electrician, or go to a building supply store or any decent bookstore to load up on do-it-yourself books on house wiring if that's what you intend to do. For those few of you who want to try alternative electrical sources (photovoltaic, hydroelectric, or wind turbine) as a primary or backup power source, you're highly likely to be working with battery banks, charge controllers, and inverters. You'll be doing most of the maintenance on them, and you'll need to know how and why they work, and how they're wired.

Photovoltaic Cells

Within a solar panel, a *cell* is the smallest structural unit capable of independent generation of electricity. A cell is made up of a sandwich of semiconductor materials, the same materials that are used in transistors. The first layer is made of phosphorous (an N-type, or negative semiconductor). The middle layer is the absorber (P-N junction). It's made of purified silicon. The third layer is made of boron (a P-type, or positive semiconductor). Each boron atom is missing an electron, and each phosphorous atom has one too many atoms. The energy of sunlight knocks some of the free phosphorous electrons off the layer, and current wants to flow as the extra electrons try to fill boron's deficit of electrons. In order to make this happen, the three middle layers are sandwiched in between two electrical contact layers that form a pathway for electron flow.

The cells are encased within a transparent material, like tempered glass on the front and a protective material on the back. Most panels are waterproofed, but there are some on the market that require the buyer to waterproof the panel with silicone around the edges of the frame, plugs, wire entries, and connections.

Each cell produces about half a volt. In a solar panel cells are wired in series to make panels with higher voltages. Your 18-watt solar panel is probably made up of 36 individual 0.5 amp cells. The total voltage and total amount of current generated is determined by the intensity of sunlight and the configuration (series versus parallel) of multiple solar panels called an *array*. The output of a solar panel in watts is determined by the rated voltage times the rated amperage. Today 12-, 24-, and 36-volt solar charging systems are the industry norm. For needs under 2 kWh, 12V is enough. A panel that is rated for a 12V system probably has an effective voltage of up to 17 volts. Larger needs will require 24 or 36V. Panels from different manufacturers can be added to the system if their voltage rate is comparable (within a volt or two).

There are basically four methods of producing solar cells:

Single crystalline is the traditional method of production and the most efficient of the four types of cells. It's also the most expensive process. The crystal is cut from a fat rod of silicon and is doped on the outside with phosphorous and the other side with boron.

Polycrystalline is also cut from a fat rod of a type of silicon that does not undergo the same cooling control or require the same purity of single crystalline silicon. The result is a matrix of many crystals. It's cheaper to produce, but since crystal boundaries tend to impede the flow of electrons, these cells are only 90 percent as efficient as single crystalline cells.

String ribbon cells are made by drawing string through liquid silicon to produce thin sheets which are then doped. These cells are cheap to produce but are only about 75 percent as efficient as single crystalline.

Amorphous or *thin film cells* are produced by vaporizing a silicon material and painting it on untempered glass or flexible stainless steel. These cells are somewhat less efficient than other types of cells and are easy to shatter. These are the cells you see on small RV and boat systems, and small panels are often sold at truck stops to trickle-charge your automotive batteries to keep them perky.

Solar cells have no storage capacity of their own. Neither do wind or water turbines. So if that's how you plan to make your electricity, you'll be storing that electricity in a 12-, 24-, or 36V battery bank. Fortunately, setting up a PV system is relatively easy. The panels themselves have no moving parts and require very little maintenance.

The total amount of radiation energy available is expressed in hours of full sunlight per square meter, or peak sun hours. This amount, also known as *insolation value*, is the average amount of sun available per day throughout the year. At "peak sun," 1,000 watts per square meter reaches the earth's surface. One full hour of peak sun provides 1,000 watts, or 1 kW per square meter. To view a map that will help you determine the insolation value at your location, type "insolation map" into your search engine on the Internet and choose from hundreds.

The performance of solar modules is rated on the percentage of solar energy they capture at sea level on a clear day. Weather, temperature, air pollution, altitude, season, dust, and anything covering the panel (i.e., snow, ice, raindrops, dust, mud) all reduce the amount of solar energy a cell will receive. Cells are most efficient at higher altitudes. But at the average altitude of earth's surface (about 2,250 feet), clean cells will receive about 85 percent. Single crystalline and polycrystalline cells only manage to convert about 10 percent of that to electrical energy, and amorphous and string ribbon cells are even less efficient.

The life of a solar cell is decades. It takes two to four years for a single or polycrystalline cell to lose 1 percent of its efficiency. Maintenance of solar panels is easy. Since there are no moving parts, you simply protect them from shattering and keep them clean.

It *is* possible to overcharge a battery and damage it. When a battery is fully charged, the current from the charging device (be it wind, solar, or hydro) should be turned off or used to charge or run another battery bank or appliance. A charge controller should be placed between the charging device and the battery bank to prevent overcharging. The controller opens the circuit to stop the flow of electricity. When the battery's charge starts to drop again, the controller closes the circuit to allow current from the charging device to serve the battery bank again. Your controller must be compatible with both the voltage of your battery bank and the amperage of your panel system.

Controllers can be simple or extremely complex. They're rated by the amps they can process from a solar array. Advanced controllers use pulse-width modulation (PWM), a process that ensures efficient charging and long battery life. Even more advanced controllers use maximum power point tracking (MPPT), a process that maximizes the amps into the battery by lowering the output voltage. As described in Ohm's Law, if the wattage doesn't change, a decrease in voltage must result in an increase in current.

Some controllers have low voltage disconnect (LVD) and battery temperature compensation (BTC). An LVD permits the connecting of loads to its terminals, which are then voltage-sensitive. If the battery voltage drops too low, the loads are automatically disconnected, resulting in decreased damage to the batteries. Batteries are temperature-sensitive. BTC adjusts the charge rate based on temperature.

It is possible to lose some of the battery charge at night and on cloudy days through a process called *reverse current*. Some solar panels come with a diode that blocks reverse current. External diodes can be added to panels that do not have their own.

As you shop for solar panels, notice the wattage ratings. Most manufacturers list the best-case rating, based on full sun and perfect conditions of sea level, temperature, and clear skies. Don't be fooled by this. Your panel will rarely function at that level for a number of reasons. First, full sun is tough to find. Even in the rural Southwest there is often enough haze in the sky on a windy but cloudless day to reduce the sunshine reaching your array. Cells get more sun at higher altitudes and in remote areas not affected by pollution.

Temperature is also a factor. Cells lose efficiency in a hot environment. If it's too warm outside for your comfort, it's probably too warm to get maximum efficiency from your array. The best defense against this is to mount your array in such a way that the backs of the panels are well ventilated and where the full array is not enclosed in a natural or artificial amphitheater that acts like a solar heater. Considering these factors, it should be obvious that solar electrical systems are going to be more successful in rural or remote, dry, high-altitude locations, which tend to be cooler, less cloudy, and less hazy.

The third and most important factor is shading and shadows. Anything placed between the cell and the sun will create a shadow and diminish the output of the panel. A small shadow has a cascading negative effect. Think of the array as a bucket, and the sunshine as a stream of water from a faucet. Your goal is to fill the bucket so full of water that it overflows. That's essentially what your array does. It fills with electricity and sends the "overflow" to the battery bank. Now . . . think about the bucket again. Along come some thirsty people who just keep filling their cups directly from the stream before it hits the bucket. The result? There's some water in the bucket, but it just doesn't fill quite enough to overflow. That's exactly what shadows and shade do to your array. With crystalline cells, a shadow the size of a basketball could shut down your entire array. There are two morals to this story: First, mount your array where it will get the best sun and the least shade—that is, perpendicular to the sun at solar noon (more on this later). Second, keep your panels clean.

Solar arrays do their best when they're set up to face at a right angle (90 degrees, or perpendicular) to the sun. You might as well fix your array so it's permanently at 90 degrees to solar noon, at an angle equal to your latitude, give or take a few degrees for winter or summer. This is easy with a clinometer (a device that measures angles of inclination) or a swing-arm protractor.

Mounting systems secure the panels in their proper position, preventing wind damage and allowing ventilation with cool air circulating behind them. There are several types of mounts available commercially, including ground or roof mounts, pole mounts, and flush mounts. Homemade mounts should be built using anodized aluminum or galvanized steel for corrosion resistance. Wood is fine, but won't last as long. Slotted steel angle stock is readily available and easy to work with. Make sure that no part of your mount will cast a shadow on the panel. Portable arrays can often be mounted on wide-base A-frame ladders or stepladders.

Adjustable tilt is nice for seasonal angle adjustments, but tracking systems that follow the sun across the sky are expensive and less effective than you would like them to be. The money would be better spent buying more panels and batteries. (For more information on mounting systems, see the appendices at the back of the book.)

Finally, solar power works very well for most appliances except large ones that use a large electric heating element (water heater, clothes dryer, electric stove, electric heater, etc.). To minimize the size of the photovoltaic system you'll need, consider using propane, natural gas, or another alternative to power these appliances.

Wind Systems

Wind power is commonly used to turn an appliance on an axis or to move an object from one location to another. Common examples are sailboats and wind turbines that generate electricity. Since this book isn't about sailing, we'll concentrate on the turbines. In a wind turbine, the wind turns a set of blades, which causes a shaft to spin. The shaft is connected to an alternator or generator that uses the rotation of the shaft to produce electricity.

Wind turbines come in two common flavors: horizontal-axis turbines, which look like a propeller with two or three blades (rotors); and vertical-axis turbines that are often described as "eggbeater" turbines. Turbines are also described as being either upwind or downwind. Upwind turbines, like most three-blade horizontal-axis turbines, are operated with the blades facing toward the wind.

Horizontal-axis turbines with larger rotor diameters catch more wind and generate more electricity than those with small rotor diameters. An average- to large-size

Two upwind, three-blade, horizontal-axis turbines. The main parts
of such a system are the rotor (propeller blade), the shaft that turns
the generator, and the nacelle that houses the generator and all the
internal parts that sit atop the tower. To the rear of the turbine is a
wind vane that orients the turbine toward the wind.

These giant turbines are located in Spanish Fork, Utah. The length of a single blade is 147 feet, and a single turbine is rated to 2.1 megawatts.

home will probably need a turbine with a rotor radius of at least 5 feet (a total wingspan of 10 feet) to generate enough electricity to be independent of the grid. Smaller turbines, called mini-turbines, have rotor radii of between 2.5 and 5 feet, and are suitable for smaller homes and vacation cabins. Transient and recreational venues (boats, RVs) can use micro-turbines, which have rotor radii of 1.5 to 2.5 feet.

It's interesting to note that small, heavy turbines (that is, turbines with all the parts densely packed into

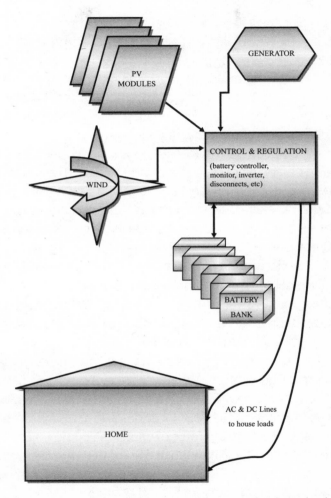

Diagram of a hybrid wind/PV system. Diagrams of various simple and complex systems can be found in the appendices in the back of the book.

a small nacelle) appear to be more durable than larger lightweight turbines (larger nacelle in comparison to rotor diameter).

Both wind and water systems are most often used as an adjunct for a PV system, often as a booster for power production in bad weather. These combination systems are referred to as *hybrid systems*.

A site that gets at least 8 mph of wind on a frequent basis can be a good site for a wind turbine. The turbines are mounted on towers, because wind increases with height. The drag at the wind-ground contact is eliminated. The difference at 100 feet may be as much as 60 percent.

Hybrid wind/PV systems include a control and regulation center with charge controller, monitor, regulator, battery bank, inverter, and disconnects. Hybrid systems often incorporate a small backup generator to reduce the number of batteries needed.

Turbines use permanent magnet alternators or coil induction generators. Whatever generator is used, the important factor will be its performance at the low wind speeds common to your location, and that will largely be determined by the rotor diameter (also known as the *swept area*) rather than the claims of the manufacturer.

So where do you mount the turbine? On a tower at least 200 feet away from wind obstacles. Remember, wind speed increases with altitude, and a 30-foot tower is considered a standard minimum. Higher is better.

Turbines are heavy and require a hefty tower that is well-guyed. The tower, turbine, and guys are assembled on the ground and then raised. Some towers for small turbines are tubular steel masts; others for larger turbines are complex framed structures. Many towers are hinged at the base for easy access. Others are constructed with gin poles, a crane-like device consisting of a vertical pole supported by guy ropes. A load (the next section of tower) is raised with a rope which goes through a pulley at the top and to a winch at the bottom.

Protect your electrical system from lightning by grounding. Be sure all the grounds in your wind and household systems are connected, giving the current a path outside your system. Also, consider a lightning arrestor, a device installed between the turbine and the battery bank, which directs excessive currents into the ground.

Water Systems

The nice thing about electricity produced from a stream is that it can work 24-7.

A simple micro-hydro system consists of a pipeline (penstock) that delivers the water to the turbine, which changes water flow to rotational energy. The alternator or generator changes rotational energy into electricity. A regulator controls the generator or diverts excess energy.

The hydroelectric systems used by homes and farms work like this: Water flow is collected into a pipeline. At the end of the pipe the water squirts out and strikes a wheel, which spins a generator, which makes electricity, which is then transmitted somewhere else by wire. The key piece to this is the *head* of the system—the distance the water falls from the collector to the turbine. The head determines the water pressure at the outlet of the pipe (pounds-per-square-inch, or psi). The pressure and the flow rate (gallons per minute) determine the amount of electricity the generator will produce. Energy can be collected from large volumes falling over small distances (low head systems), or small volumes falling over large distances (high head systems). Obviously the most effective sites are going to be in the watercourses of the mountains. Any site which could support a pipeline that gives 10 psi—or at least 20 to 30 feet of head delivering at least 2 gallons per minute—can produce substantial electricity.

DC generators are typically used for smaller residential systems, and AC generators are usually used for larger commercial systems. High-flow, low-head sites and AC sites are complicated and expensive.

An impulse turbine functions by using the impact of a spray of water from a nozzle or jet, also at the end of the pipeline. It sprays onto little cups on the turbine wheel. Kinetic energy from the water spins the wheel (runner). There are several impulse turbines available.

Sites with at least 150 feet of head are best served by a Pelton wheel impulse turbine. The Pelton is a wheel on an axis that's perpendicular to the flow of the current. Cups attached to the wheel catch the spurting water and cause the wheel to spin, which spins the turbine. Axial flow turbines are like propellers, with the rotors spinning on an axis that's parallel to the flow of water. Pelton wheels are the best choice for high-pressure, low-volume systems (in other words, the typical mountain trickle). A Pelton system like this can be put in place for as little as $1,000.

The low voltage generated by micro-hydro systems is difficult to transmit in large quantities or over long distances. The battery bank should be as close as possible to the turbine. If the distance between the batteries and the turbine is over 100 feet, a 24- or 48-volt system will probably work better than a 12-volt system. Extreme distances will require larger-gauge wire and specialized technical expertise.

Micro-hydro systems require special charge controllers or regulators. Their controllers divert excess power to a secondary load, usually a water or space heater. These diversion controllers can be used with wind turbines or PV cells, but solar controllers cannot be used with micro-hydro or wind systems.

To get started setting up a micro-hydro system, a few measurements are needed. First, the head; this is the difference in altitude between the collection point and the turbine. The easiest ways to measure this are with a topographic map (7.5 minute series) or with a GPS, or both. When using GPS for altitude, make sure the device has acquired at least three satellites to ensure accuracy. If pipe has already been installed between the collection point and the turbine site, use a pressure gauge at the turbine site and multiply the reading by 2.31 (feet of head = psi x 2.31).

Assuming the pipe has already been installed between the collection point and the turbine site, time how long it takes water from the pipe to fill a 5-gallon bucket. Divide the time by 5, then divide that into 60. This gives you the flow in gallons per minute. For example, if it takes 90 seconds to fill the 5-gallon bucket, divide 5 into 90 to get 18. Then divide 18 into 60 to get 3.33 gallons per minute (gpm).

Sizing Your System

To figure out how big a system needs to be, you first need to determine how many watts you'll be using and the amount of time those watts are used (watt-hours). You can then compare those figures to the amount of energy resources (sun, wind, water head, and flow, available at your geographic location). Use this information to determine the size and number of components you'll need to provide the amount of power you require (some system-sizing instructions are included in the appendices in the back of the book).

Finally, let's repeat the obvious: The size of your system can be drastically reduced by taking a few conservation measures. Use energy-efficient lighting and appliances, and consider nonelectric alternatives.

Batteries

Batteries, or battery banks, are required by all stand-alone and utility interface systems. The two most common rechargeable battery types are nickel-cadmium (NiCad) and lead-acid (L-A) batteries. Lead-acid batteries have plates of lead submerged in sulfuric acid. NiCad batteries have plates of nickel and cadmium in a potassium hydroxide solution.

Lead-acid batteries are the cheapest, and readily available. They come in several sizes and designs, but the most important thing to look for when choosing L-A batteries is the depth of the charging cycle.

Shallow-cycle batteries (car batteries) give high current for short periods. They do not tolerate repeated deep discharging (below 20 percent), so are not suitable for PV systems.

Deep-cycle batteries are made to be repeatedly discharged by as much as 80 percent. Even so, these batteries will have a longer life if they're cycled shallow.

Try to stay above 50 percent capacity. All L-A batteries fail early if they're not recharged after each cycle. A long-discharged L-A battery is subject to sulfation of the positive plate and permanent loss of capacity. An electronic desulfater can be added to extend the battery life.

Nickel-cadmium batteries are expensive, but can last many times longer than L-A batteries. NiCads can be 100 percent discharged and can stay discharged without damaging their capacity. Also, their capacity does not decrease in cold temperatures and they are not damaged by freezing. The voltage is stable from full charge to discharge. Because of these factors, smaller batteries can be used.

NiCad charging efficiency is the same as L-A batteries, and their self-discharge rate is very slow. They require a higher voltage (16 to 17 volts for a 12V battery) than L-A batteries to bring them to a full charge. Many AC battery chargers cannot provide the higher voltage, but some solar panels do. Note that some 12-volt inverters may shut down temporarily with a battery at that voltage.

Additional NiCads can be added at any time to the bank. L-A banks will "dumb down" to match the least-efficient or weakest battery in the bank.

Nickel-iron batteries have charge and discharge voltages, life, and cold-temperature performance similar to NiCad batteries. However, they don't deliver the high amperage that NiCads do, so a larger battery will be needed for the same power. One other advantage of these batteries is that they are made without lead or cadmium.

A typical L-A battery contains liquid acid in cells that are not sealed. They can leak. Gel-cell, AGM, and sealed lead-acid are terms for batteries that are alternative choices in place of the traditional L-A battery.

A *gel-cell* uses acid in a semisolid gel form and is therefore less likely to leak. The disadvantage is that a coating can develop on the battery plates, which reduces performance.

Absorbent glass mat (AGM) batteries use internal glass mats to soak up the acid. There's a slightly higher chance of leakage from cracks with AGM than with gel-cell, but AGMs deliver a more consistent performance.

A *sealed lead-acid* battery can be any battery that uses lead-acid for electrolytes and is sealed. This includes both gel-cell and AGM batteries. The obvious advantages of sealed batteries are that the battery fluid is less likely to leak and does not have to be replaced. They are virtually maintenance-free.

The size of a battery bank is determined by the storage capacity required, the maximum discharge rate, and the minimum temperature at the bank site (for L-A batteries). At 40 degrees F, L-A batteries will only function at 75 percent of capacity, and at 0 degrees F, at 50 percent.

Storage capacity is expressed in amp-hours. The battery bank should have enough amp-hours capacity to supply needed power during a long period of cloudy weather. Add another 20 percent for L-A batteries. If there's a backup source of power, such as a generator and battery charger, the battery bank can be smaller. See Appendix 4 for more detailed instructions on sizing your battery bank.

Charge Controllers

Let's summarize what we know about charge controllers: When a battery is fully charged, the current from the charging device should be turned off or used to charge or run another battery bank or appliance. A charge controller should be placed between the charging device and the battery bank to prevent overcharging. The controller opens the circuit to stop the flow of electricity. When the battery's charge starts to drop again, the controller closes the circuit to allow current from the charging device to serve the battery bank again. The controller must be compatible with both the voltage of the battery bank and the amperage of the charging device system

Controllers are rated by the amps they can process from a solar array. Advanced controllers use pulse-width modulation (PWM), a process that ensures efficient charging and long battery life. More advanced controllers use maximum power point tracking (MPPT), a process that maximizes the amps into the battery by lowering the output voltage.

A low voltage disconnect LVD permits the connecting of loads to its terminals, which are then voltage-sensitive. If the battery voltage drops too low, the loads are automatically disconnected, resulting in decreased damage to the batteries. Batteries are temperature-sensitive. Battery temperature compensation (BTC) adjusts the charge rate based on temperature.

"Monitor" or "regulator" units are charge controllers with additional bells and whistles. Typically they will include an ammeter for current measurement, adjustable voltage set points, and LED lights to show charge status.

Inverters

Inverters convert DC in batteries to on-demand AC through a process of transforming, filtering, and stepping voltages (changing them from one level to another). The more processing that happens, the cleaner the output, but this comes at the expense of conversion efficiency. When you shop for an inverter, you'll choose based on the following factors:

- Maximum continuous load. Inverters are rated by maximum continuous watt output.
- Maximum surge load. Asking an inverter for more power than it can give will simply shut it down

or cook it. If your inverter will be expected to run induction motors (e.g., washer and dryer, dishwasher, large power tools, etc.), you will need a surge capacity of three to seven times that of the highest appliance wattage. For example, if your air conditioner runs at 1,500 watts, you'll need about 5,000 watts of surge capacity to get the motor started.

- Input battery voltage (12, 24, or 48V).
- The output voltage needed (120 versus 240). If 240 volts is needed, either a transformer is added or two identical inverters are series-stacked to produce 240V.
- Purity of the AC waveform required.
- Whether you need a static inverter or a synchronous inverter. A synchronous inverter changes DC to AC and feeds it directly to the consumer on demand. Any excess power is fed into the grid (the utility company), which acts as a storage battery. When you need extra power, you take it back from the grid. These are also called grid intertie inverters.
- Optional features.

Inverters deliver current in one of three basic waveforms: square wave, modified square wave (modified sine wave), and pure sine wave (true sine wave). The closest waveform to grid waveform is pure sine wave.

Square wave inverters are inexpensive but also relatively inefficient. Modified square wave inverters allow greater surge capacity to start motors, but also allow economic power for running small appliances and electronics. Most appliances will accept them. However, they may damage or fail to run some printers and copiers and some rechargeable tools. They also cause a buzz in audio equipment, fans, and fluorescent lights. Pure sine wave inverters are the choice for running equipment that is sensitive to waveforms.

Some inverters have special features. An example is an internal battery charger that can rapidly charge batteries when an AC source is connected to the inverter input terminals. Another example is automated transfer switching, which enables switching from one AC source to another or from utility power to inverter power for designated loads. Other possible features are battery temperature compensation, internal relays to control loads, and automatic remote generator start-stop.

Note that efficiency losses between the source, wires, batteries, and inverter can be as high as 25 percent.

Power Centers

A power center is a panel into which the inverter, charge controller, safety disconnects, lightning arrestors, breakers, and system meters are mounted. For larger alternative energy systems, a power center is definitely advantageous.

Switches

A switch is a device used to break or open an electric circuit or to divert current from one conductor to another. This general category includes timers, switches, and relays. Some of the switches you might be working with include circuit breakers, transfer switches, power panel breakers, and auto transfer switches.

Connections

The clear standard for today's home-sized solar arrays are the MC connectors. MC stands for multi-contact, and the MC is a proprietary switch that has male and female ends and comes with various cable sizes. They provide clean, code-compliant, weather-tight connections. MC1 has been in common use, but the trend is toward the MC2 connector because it's considered a better connection, and is now required by most building codes. There are adapter kits for going from MC1 to MC2. The small panels you often find at truck stops, auto parts stores, and boat shops often use what are called universal connectors, or SAE connectors.

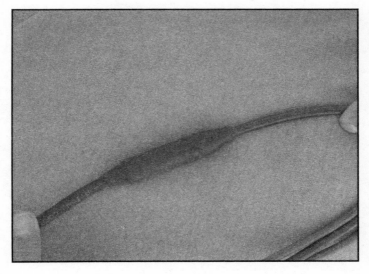

An MC connector.

Electrical Safety Devices

Two of the most important safety components are good enclosures and overcurrent protection. Enclosures have many uses including a wiring point for energy sources, weather protection for overcurrent devices, and load disconnection. Overcurrent devices and switch gear provide safe means to disconnect power. Overcurrent devices include fuses, fuse blocks, and circuit breakers. Consult an electrician about electrical safety devices for your system.

Wiring the System

First and foremost, make sure the batteries are matched to the voltage capabilities of the charge controller and the inverter (12V, 24V, 48V). Batteries and panels are similarly wired in series to achieve the correct voltage, and in parallel to achieve the correct current (amps).

Series connections are made by connecting a pair of opposite poles or terminals of different batteries or PV panels (negative to positive). This increases the total voltage. The voltages are added together, while the amp capacity remains the same as just one of the batteries or panels.

Parallel connections are made by connecting the same poles or terminals (positive to positive and negative to negative) of multiple panels or batteries. The amperages are added together, but the voltage stays the same as one of the batteries or panels, or as one of the parallel battery or panel strings in a bank or array.

Battery banks often have batteries connected in both series and parallel.

Batteries are easy to wire when they're set in neat rows on long shelves. Make sure there's enough room above the battery to be able to access the caps to check and add water. Batteries can also be placed and oriented in different directions to fit tight or

Portable emergency 12V system with two batteries in parallel and two, 1-amp 15-volt panels in parallel, making a 12V, 30W system. In this parallel PV panel array, all the red wires (+) are connected to the red controller wire, and all black (-) wires are connected to the black controller wire. The battery terminals in such a system would be connected with cables or jumper bars. Here the red terminals are connected to each other, the black terminals to each other, and the positive (red) and negative (black) outputs are taken from terminals on the opposite ends of the bank. Pulling the main output cables from opposite corners of the bank ensures that all the batteries in the bank are charged and discharged equally. This rig is mounted on a dolly for portability. Note the charge controller mounted to the front of the upper battery box, and a 400-watt, two-receptacle inverter mounted on top of the same box.

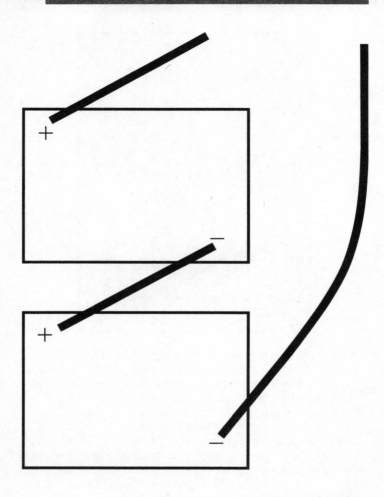

Power sources (batteries and solar panels) wired in series. The amperage stays the same, but the voltages are added. These two 12V, 120-amp batteries wired in series produce 24V at 120 amps.

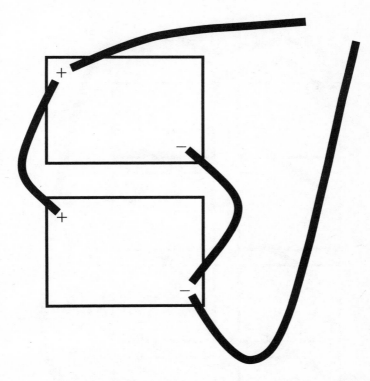

Batteries or solar panels wired in parallel. The voltage stays the same. The amps are added. These two 12V, 120-amp batteries wired in parallel produce 12 volts at 240 amps. Note that in parallel systems, the main cables must come from opposite corners to ensure that batteries are charged and discharged equally.

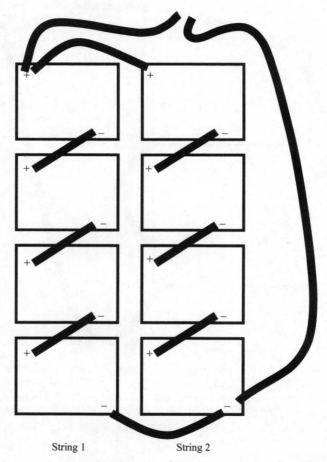

String 1   String 2

To increase both amperage and voltage, batteries or solar panels can be configured with strings of series batteries wired in parallel. This shows a 48V, 240-amp system made with 12V, 120-amp batteries.

odd-shaped areas. However they are arranged, make sure the jumper cables or jumper bars don't obstruct the caps or threaten to contact the wrong terminal. (For more information on wire and cable use and capacity, see the appendices in the back of the book.)

CHAPTER 5
Leaving the Grid: Water

Even with global warming and the droughts we've experienced over the past decade, water in North America is plentiful, and as long as you don't waste it, there's plenty for any off-gridder in the form of groundwater and precipitation.

Some folks are fortunate enough to have direct access to lakes and streams, and they can take water easily by gravity, siphon systems, or pumps. Others of us aren't that lucky, and we'll use the next dozen pages or so to describe what we can do to get our share.

In my primary home, with three residents, I average about five gallons per day for cooking and drinking. Maybe twice that for bathing and laundry, and twice again for keeping the garden growing and my xeric landscape looking healthy. My neighbor, on the other hand, waters her enormous lawn and timbered landscape full-throttle for as long as twenty hours a day. With the drought still burning southeast Utah into bits of crispy dust, it seems unusually sinful. Her response to my complaints: "It's well water, so I can do what I want. God will provide."

Here's what the U.S. Geological Survey says about well-users wasting water: "If you own a water-table well and you pump excessive amounts of water from your well, there is a danger of your well going dry as consumption continues and groundwater levels fall. Since aquifers can be quite extensive, the usage of your well can influence other people miles away. Groundwater that supplies your well also feeds streams during periods of low flow, so pumping from your well may also cause the water levels in streams to be lower." If you'd like to read more, go to: http://md.water.usgs.gov/faq/drought.html#GW05.

It's time to stop being greedy with water. The earth has to take care of a huge, expanding population. Your access to well water does not entitle you to unlimited wastefulness.

Conserving Water

In the chapter on conservation I mentioned several ways to conserve water. Let's emphasize a few points here:

- Fewer flushes.
- Repair leaking toilets and faucets immediately.
- Wash only full loads of laundry.

- Use filtered or treated gray water for gardens and landscapes.
- Don't overwater.

Wells

Since we're on the subject, let's talk about wells. A well is a hole dug to the water table or an aquifer (see the glossary for definitions), and a pump or other system to draw the water out. Like anything else, wells are highly regulated by the offices of local and state government, especially the health department. A badly done well can leak some nasty contaminants into the local water system. Also, wells are generally not cheap to sink, and you'll probably be wanting a deep well, since the deeper the well, the more likely you are to get truly clean water. Even then, you'll probably end up filtering the water to make sure. So, bottom line: Use a licensed well-driller and get it done right. And when deciding how and where to do your well, get some insight from the farmers and older residents nearby.

If you're lucky enough to have access to the perfect well-drilling site—for instance, a water table 20 feet down, in deep loam or sandy clay with few rocks and no nearby contamination potential—it's quite possible to hand-drive the well. Here's how it's done: To limit the pumping that will have to be done between the well and the house, find a site as close to the house as possible. The site must be at least 100 feet away from and uphill of any source of contamination, such as an outhouse, animal stables, or septic systems. Use a 1.25-inch to 2-inch well point (drive point). A well point is a pipe, usually 18 to 60 inches long, with openings large enough to allow water to enter. The size of the openings depends on the sediment matrix holding the water. The finer the sediment, the smaller the holes will need to be. Holes should let finer particles in but keep large particles out.

Pound the well head down into the soil with a maul. When you need more length, remove the hammering cap, clean the threads, and screw on a new riser pipe (5 to 6 feet in length, with a 6-inch nipple) using some monkey wrenches and with a little joint or pipe thread compound in the threads. Start pounding again and repeat the process. Special drive couplings may be needed during this process to keep the impact off the threads.

There are abundant websites with suggestions for determining whether your well point has entered water-bearing ground. If you reach an artesian source with some pressure, you might get water gushing up through the pipe. Otherwise, you'll have to attach a suction pump to bring up the water.

Boring a well in rock-free soil is possible with a hand-turned auger, but the process is immensely labor-intensive. Posthole augers can be driven by a power head and pressurized with water to soften and clear out the hole.

Keep in mind that you can use the hand-drawing method to bring up water from a well if it's deeper than 200 feet. A suction pump, on the other hand, will not work with water more than 20 feet down. For deeper wells you'll probably use a submerged push-type electric pump (possibly solar or wind-powered), or a windmill.

Hand-digging a wide shaft and finishing it with a windlass was the traditional way of creating a well years ago. This method is not practical or safe, especially if the shaft is deeper than the diggers are tall and the soil is unconsolidated. Shaft collapse is a common hazard. Get advice and experienced help.

Springs

A spring is an upwelling of water at the ground's surface. That includes shallow seepages from nearby collectors, natural or unnatural (including lakes, streams, aquifers, saturated sediment, waste dumps). If you intend to use stream water, you absolutely must have it comprehensively tested at a laboratory. The good news is that natural sediments and soil organisms do an excellent job of keeping water clean, but they can become overloaded with heavy or repeated contamination. Pollutants in your test results may mean you need to change sources and go deeper for cleaner water. You may find pesticides from the farm next door, and E. coli or increased phosphates indicate contamination with sewage.

Finding a spring is often easier than it sounds. A good time to look is during the early spring months, in periods of high snowmelt or heavy rain. Watch for small runnels emptying into roadside ditches or otherwise dry canyons or arroyos, and follow them to their sources. Check back monthly and watch the progression of the local vegetation. If it remains green, or the ground remains wet year-round, there's a spring there. Many springs are little more than seeps.

If you live in a wooded area, look for wide, indented lines in the ground. This indicates a channel of some kind, either above or below ground. Seeps will produce a muddy basin or a small pond. The presence of marsh plants growing there in dark soil means a spring is present. It's okay if the marsh stinks a bit; you're going to have the water tested anyway, and smell isn't necessarily an indicator of serious contamination.

Once the spring has been located, it needs to be cleaned out and prepared. It's easier to wait until the surrounding area is at its driest before digging out the stagnant sediment (which, again, may have an unpleasant smell). The water that feeds the spring comes from subsurface saturation or from subsurface flows in the deeper sediment or cracks in the bedrock.

The object is to dig out enough to locate this clean source. Then gravel and perforated pipe are put down to collect the water, and a dam of compacted soil, plastic sheeting, or concrete is built downstream of the source, to force the water into the pipe. The pipe is run to a spring box to collect, settle out dirt and sand, and protect the water from contamination. Read about building spring boxes at http://www.cee.mtu.edu/peacecorps/documents_july03/springbox_FINAL.pdf.

Here are some simple instructions to help you maintain the spring:

- Keep livestock and other potential pollutants and polluters away from the spring.
- Divert surface water, which can contain contaminating sediments, away from the box by digging diversion channels well uphill from it.
- Clean the settling basin out twice each year, or at least once each spring.
- Fix leaks in the pipes or spring box.
- Do not allow the overflow pipe to clog.

Once you've got a spring, how do you tap it? By bucket is the easiest way, but for most of us, that's a bit harsh. If the spring is located upslope from the house, the water can be moved through a gravity-flow system to a font, a cistern, or a water tank at the house. The font, cistern, or tank drain should be configured to allow overages of clean water to drain back into the streambed. Bales of hay or straw (or dirt), placed over the box, will help prevent freezing; also, allowing some water to run from the box will retard freezing.

Harvesting Precipitation: Catchment Systems

A water catchment system (aka, surface-water containment system, rain-harvesting storage system, run-off catchment system) is an attractive alternative where groundwater is contaminated, wells can't be dug, springs can't be found, or where rainwater is low. These types of systems have been in use for thousands of years in countries with poor groundwater resources. Even in the desert, a short rain can deliver enough water to keep the household going until the next storm.

The most common form of storm harvesting is a simple rain barrel, fed by the downspout of the rain gutters or eaves of the building. There's a huge inventory of commercial rain barrels to choose from, some with their own roof-cleaner diverters (they divert the roof water until the roof has been rinsed off). By the way, metal or clay-tile roofs seem to be cleaner than shingled roofs. If you have a shingled roof, you'll want a roof-cleaner diverter and perhaps a pre-filter in the system before the water enters the storage device.

The water from a barrel is not pressurized, but can be used to water a garden via a hose from the barrel drain. Elevating the barrel (commonly on cinder blocks) a bit increases the pressure, but it won't support a plumbing system of any kind without a pump. Storm-harvesting systems that are intended to provide water for drinking, cooking, and bathing will need pumping, filtration, and disinfection systems.

The harvesting system may also drain into larger above-ground tanks, into below-ground cisterns, or into dammed reservoirs, some commercial versions of which also have roof cleaners.

Aside from roofs, melt- and rainwater can be captured from gullies and washes, but the obvious problem is sediment (mud) buildup and the control of raging floodwaters. Large systems like this can become hazards to anything downstream.

A cistern is basically just a tank, made of concrete, steel, fiberglass, or plastic, that sits above or below ground. If your cistern or water tank is above ground and higher than your building's internal plumbing, you can use the weight of the water in the cistern for water pressure. Otherwise, a pump is needed to send water from the catchment to the house. Again, filtering and disinfection will be needed before using the water for drinking, cooking, or bathing.

If you're using a rain barrel or any other above-ground storage device, remember to take steps to keep it from freezing.

This 33-gallon garbage-can collector runs 50 to 75 feet of downslope soaker hose for almost three hours. The gutter drain is placed in the hole in the top of the lid to catch runoff. The screen beneath the lid keeps mosquitoes from breeding. The valve at the bottom allows the hose to be turned on and off. Cost: $18, not including hose.

Testing Your Water

Test any off-grid water before you drink it. If you can't test it first, you can use a combination of methods to treat and purify it: water treatment tablets from the local sporting goods store, or household bleach (sodium hypochlorite, 3 to 6 percent) at a ratio of 1 teaspoon to 5 gallons of water.

Lab samples for testing for microorganisms, including Giardia cysts, and chemicals need to be fresh (less than twenty-four hours old). Use an independent testing service to do the tests. Comprehensive testing will cost a couple of hundred dollars. The local health department will be able to have the testing done for less, but getting the HD involved may be a mistake. If they shut you down, it could be nearly impossible to get them "uninvolved."

Water-Source Hygiene

Pay attention to what's happening around your water source and its watershed. Watch for dead animals, contamination by human sewage, and chemical contamination.

Filter your water. Consider putting a filter/chlorinator system at the well head and installing purifiers on or before the faucets that will be used for drinking and cooking water. When it comes to filters, you generally get what you pay for. Expect to fork out some dollars for a good system and be aware that high-tech filtering systems require periodic filter replacement and water testing.

Water Heating Devices

Storage or tank-type water heaters are the most common in the American home. They are usually 20- to 80-gallon capacity, and fueled by electricity, propane, oil, or natural gas. These units heat up water in an insulated tank and provide a large amount of water for a short period of time. The disadvantage of these units is that they use energy even when not in operation. The life expectancy of a tank is ten to fifteen years, but can be increased by replacing the tank's internal anode rod.

Heat Pump Heaters

These units use a heater/compressor and refrigerant fluid to transfer heat from one place to another. They are fueled by electricity, but the heat source is warm air in the vicinity of the heat pump. For this reason heat pumps work best in warm climates. They use less electricity because it takes less energy to move heat than to create it. They are available with built-in water tanks called *integral units*, or as add-ons to existing water heaters. They are expensive and complicated to install, so it's best to hire a contractor for this job.

Indirect Water Heaters

Indirect water heaters use the home heating system's boiler. Hot water is stored in a separate insulated tank. Heat is transferred from the boiler via a small circulation pump and heat exchanger.

Disadvantages include the fact that it's an integral part of the home heating system and that it's usually easiest to install during new building construction by a contractor.

On-Demand or Tankless Heaters

These heaters only go to work when the water is turned on and reaches a minimum flow rate. A gas flame or heater element switches on, heating water as it passes through a radiator-like heat exchanger. These heaters do not store hot water. Tankless water heaters may include many safety features; for example, a certain flow rate may be required in order for the device to turn on; temperature and pressure-relief valves; and additional heat sensors on the heat exchanger, to mention a few.

The flow rate itself is limited by the heating capacity of the device. It allows hot water to flow at limited gallons per minute, and increased flow decreases the temperature of the water. At a moderate rate, hot water runs out only when the gas or the water runs out. Most models are fueled by natural gas or propane. Electric models are available but use excessive amounts of electricity. This type of water heater is a good choice for small homes.

Solar Water Heaters

Solar water heaters (SWH) can be very expensive but there is a quick return on the investment. They tend to be about three times as efficient at harvesting and processing the energy from the sun as photovoltaic systems. There are several types of solar water heater systems, and they work differently depending on the climate. Simple systems are best. All the bells and whistles, sensors, and valves tend to break down. Basic heaters use passive designs with sunlight and heat as the controls.

Getting Started with Solar Water Heating

- Learn how to conserve energy.
- Reduce your energy losses by increasing the number of your energy-efficient appliances and decreasing your overall consumption of electricity.
- Insulate your water heater with a jacket and insulate your hot-water pipes.
- Immediately fix leaking hot-water faucets.

Many of today's texts seem to make solar water heating sound very complicated. The intent of this book is to explain things for the layperson in the simplest terms, providing information about what's available. First, I'll explain the basic terminology (much of which has already been explained in chapter 5); next, I'll briefly describe the standard components of SWH systems; and then I'll describe the actual systems themselves.

Basic Terminology of Solar Water Heating Systems

Active versus passive: Active systems use moving parts (like pumps and valves). Passive systems have no moving parts.

Heat exchanger: A device which transfers heat through a conducting wall from one fluid to another.

Integrated Collector Storage (ICS): The combination of collector and storage tank in one unit (also referred to as "batch").

Open-loop versus closed-loop: In open-loop systems (also called direct systems), the domestic water is heated directly by the collector. In closed-loop systems (often called indirect systems), a heat transfer fluid called a solar fluid is heated by the collector, and then the heat is transferred from the solar fluid to the domestic water via a heat exchanger.

Solar fluid: This is the fluid used within closed-loop or indirect systems. It's usually distilled water or an anti-freeze-and-water mixture.

Thermosiphon: A fancy term referring to the natural convective movement of a liquid due to differences in temperature. As you'll see below, it allows water or solar fluid to move within a circuit without using a mechanical pump.

Components of Solar Water Heating Systems

Components of SWH systems include the following:

- collector
- collector mount
- storage tank
- water pump
- heat exchanger
- expansion tank
- controls
- isolation and tempering valves
- backup water heater

Note that not all components are required for all systems. The simpler the system and the fewer the components, the less chance there will be of component failure and the easier the system will be to maintain.

Collectors

Batch Collectors, or Integrated Collector Storage (ICS) Devices

In these systems, the hot-water storage tank is the solar absorber. The tank is painted black or has a special coating and is mounted in an insulated box, usually about 6 inches deep, that has glass on one side. Cold water is piped to the bottom of the tank. Sun shines through the glass, heats up on the black surface, and warms the water inside the tank. Warmed water is taken from the top of the tank when a hot faucet is opened and cold water again moves into the tank. Some are single large tanks (30 gallons or more), and others use several metal tubes plumbed in a series. Single tanks are usually made of steel. Tubes are usually made of copper. Tube-type tanks perform better because more surface area is exposed, but they also cool off more quickly at night. ICS tanks can reach temperatures as high as 180° F on a warm sunny day, and half that on a warm cloudy day.

There are some disadvantages to batch collectors. They are extremely heavy when full and must be mounted on sturdy structures (a reinforced roof or on the ground). When mounted the collectors must be tilted so they will drain properly. Batch heaters are good to use in climates that do not freeze. They can be used in seasonal homes during the warm months, but must be drained before it freezes.

Flat Plate Collectors (FPCs)

Flat plate collector heaters are the most commonly used throughout the world. They are durable and effective, and they shed snow and ice. FPCs are shallow, rectangular boxes, usually 4 feet by 8 feet by 4 to 6 inches, consisting of a strong frame, glass on the front of the collector, and a solid back. Just beneath the glass is an absorber plate with copper pipe manifolds that run across the top and bottom of the collector inside the frame. Smaller riser tubes are welded perpendicular along the manifold, spaced about 4 to 5 inches apart. A flat copper fin is welded or soldered to a riser to transfer heat from the fin to the tube. The fin is painted or coated with a special material to maximize absorption. FPCs need a strong mount (usually aluminum) to withstand high winds. All components of the collector must be made of compatible metals to reduce corrosion.

Low-iron, low-glare tempered glass is commonly used for glazing FPCs. A rubberized gasket along the edge of the frame ensures a proper seal and protects the frame.

Evacuated tubes: This evacuated tube system at Valley of the Gods B&B provides hot water for the owners and four guest rooms.

Evacuated Tube Collectors (ETCs)

In an ETC an annealed glass vacuum tube surrounds each individual pipe or absorber plate. The vacuum allows higher temperatures to develop. Some types have the tube connected to a manifold so water circulates through the tube. Other tubes contain a special fluid that evaporates and rises to a heat exchanger. When it cools off, it condenses and falls back into the tube. Still other tubes have a metal rod attached to the absorber and protruding from the tube for insertion into a manifold where circulating water picks up the heat.

The disadvantages of ETCs include the fact that they can generate temperatures above boiling (causing scald injuries and system-pressure hazards). These problems can be mitigated by oversizing the storage tank, undersizing the collector, or by using a drain-back system (see below). The tubes are very fragile, and the collectors do not shed snow and ice well.

Concentrating Collectors

These use a reflective parabolic surface to concentrate energy to a focal point where the absorber is located. To be effective the collector must track the sun. It can reach high temperatures, but the technology has not yet been developed for domestic water heating systems.

Pool Collectors

Plain and simple, this book isn't about swimming pools. It's about achieving the necessities of life by becoming involved in off-grid technology. If you have a swimming pool, you can afford to ask a technician or consultant and dealer about heating your pool with solar power. In the meantime, simply type "solar pool heaters" in your search engine to locate several websites that will have the basic information you need to get started.

Collector Mounts

Collector mounting systems—or racks, as they're often called—are installed as roof mounts, awning mounts, or ground mounts. Roof mounts are done on brackets a few inches above and parallel to the roof. Ground mounts are basically four posts with lengths adjusted for tilt. Awning mounts attach the collector to a wall and use vertical supports to push the collector out for tilt. Collectors full of fluid or water can be enormously heavy. If weight is an issue, ground mounts are easiest and least likely to cause structural damage to the home.

Solar Storage Tanks

A solar storage tank is an insulated water tank. Cold water from your regular water heater enters, and solar-heated water exits. In closed-loop systems the water is heated by contact with a coil of pipe containing water or antifreeze that circulates through the collectors. In open-loop systems the water is directly circulated through the collectors. The solar preheated water is then plumbed back to the cold side of the water heater, which now functions as a backup heater. When a hot-water tap is

(A)

(B)

(C)

The solar water heating system at a laundromat. The panels (A) contain evacuated tubes, with manifold (B), shown disassembled; and a large storage tank (C).

opened, preheated water is moved from the solar tank to the backup heater.

Water Pump

The water within a system has to move by some means, either by a natural method (convection, gravity, natural pressure) or by mechanical pump (or circulator). An AC (plug-in) or DC (photovoltaic) pump can be used to move water or antifreeze between the collector and the storage tank. The size of the pump depends on the distance and elevation difference between the collector and the tank. Mechanical pumps are not used in passive systems (batch and thermosiphon systems).

Heat Exchanger

This is a device used in closed-loop systems to transfer heat from one fluid to another without mixing the fluids. In storage tanks, some heat exchangers are placed inside the tank (internal), and are often just a coil of metal tubing or pipe in the bottom of the tank. Or the exchanger may be wrapped around the outside of the tank (external) underneath the insulation and cover. External exchangers are often pipes within pipes, with solar fluid in one and water in the other, flowing in opposite directions. The flow is produced by pump or by thermosiphoning (convection), or a combination of both.

Expansion Tanks

An expansion tank stores air in a bladder or diaphragm. A certain operating pressure for the system is set by the owner. The pipes and system are filled with solar fluid that occupies a specific volume within a certain temperature range. As the fluid gets hotter and expands, the tank compensates by allowing the fluid to compress the air in the bladder or diaphragm, thus keeping the fluid pressure within a safe level. Even with temperatures near boiling, the system doesn't explode, and it remains a beautiful day in the neighborhood.

The size of the tank depends on the amount of fluid the system carries (the number and size of the collectors and the length and diameter of the pipes in the solar loop). It's normally about 3 to 6 gallons for a typical home. Usually a 2-gallon tank (#15) is sufficient for home use (a #30 tank has twice the capacity). Expansion tanks are required by closed-loop systems.

Differential Controls

In active systems, when the collector is hotter than the tank, the pump circulates fluids. But when the tank is hotter than the collector, the pump must be shut down. That's the job of the differential control. This can actually be accomplished by a couple of different devices. A differential thermostat compares the temperature of the collector and tank and switches off and on accordingly. A PV pump is simpler: It comes on when the sun comes out, and as the sun gets brighter, the pump runs faster. When the sun goes down, the pump stops. Differential controls are not needed in batch or thermosiphon systems.

Isolation Valve (Solar Bypass)

This type of bypass valve can be placed to isolate the solar tank in case of a problem or to bypass the backup water heater if the solar water heater can meet all the needs of the household. The valve is used to direct the flow either through or past the solar tank or backup heater.

When used to isolate the solar tank, one or more are placed in the incoming and outgoing lines to the water tank. The valve(s) still allows the backup water heater to remain in service.

An isolation valve may be in a three-valve configuration, or a three-port, two-valve.

Tempering Valve

A tempering (or mixing) valve goes at the end of the system, before the faucet, to prevent scalding burns. If the water is too hot, the valve opens to mix in cold water. The preferred temperature can be set by the user directly on the valve.

Backup Water Heater

This heater runs on electricity, natural gas, propane, or even wood fuel. It ensures hot water whether the sun shines or not, boosting the temperature of solar pre-heated or unheated water to the preferred temperature settings. The backup can be a tank or tankless heater.

Different Types of Solar Water Heating Systems

Screw on your thinking caps—this is where it gets a little complicated. If you need a review of simple physics, go back and read chapter 4 again.

Batch (ICS) Systems

The simplest, least-expensive, and easiest to install are batch (ICS) systems. These open-loop, passive, direct-heating systems are usually plumbed between the cold-water supply and a conventional water heater. Whenever a hot-water faucet is opened, cold water flows into the batch collector and pushes the hot water out of it and into the backup water heater. The backup adds only enough heat to achieve the temperature that has been preset by the owner.

The most complete batch system could be as simple as a batch collector and pipes. Crude batch collectors are fairly easy to make, and there are do-it-yourself plans all over the Internet.

Thermosiphon Systems (TS)

These systems are driven by convective currents. To put it more simply, heat rises, causing a current. In moderate climates an open-loop TS can be used in which cold domestic water is piped into the bottom of the collector; as it heats up, it rises to the top of the collector. In colder climates a solar solution of antifreeze and water is used in a closed-loop system. Since the collector is likely to be roof-mounted, freeze-proof piping (such as PEX, cross-linked polyethylene) can be used on the roof and in the attic. The heated water is stored in a well-insulated tank so there's no overnight heat loss.

Open-Loop Direct Systems

Open-loop direct systems are the simplest of the active systems. Unfortunately, they can only be used in areas that don't freeze hard. The system consists of a large solar collector and a large storage tank. Often a standard water heater tank is used without the heater element hooked up. The storage tank holds the preheated water and feeds a backup water heater. An automatic or manually operated air vent installed at the high point of the collector is used to purge air before the system gets started. The circulating pump, which can be a simple 10-watt PV pump or an AC (plug-in) pump with thermostatic control, can be used to move the water or fluid. A device called a snap-switch sensor can be installed to limit the temperature in the tank. When this spring-loaded device senses a predetermined temperature, it snaps (rotates) 90 degrees and breaks the circuit to stop the pump.

Pressurized Solar Fluid (Glycol) Systems

These are active closed-loop systems. Domestic water is sent to a storage tank but not to a collector. A water and antifreeze mixture circulates through the collectors and then through a pipe-coil heat exchanger in the storage tank, then back through the collector. The domestic water is warmed by conductive heat transfer from the coil.

The solar fluid sent through the collector is usually a mix of water and glycol that prevents freezing; the warmer the climate, the smaller the proportion of glycol used. Antifreeze does have some disadvantages over water, so the smallest proportion possible should be used.

These systems require an expansion tank and additional components for venting and routing. Their advantage is that the collector can be mounted anywhere without fear of it freezing.

Closed-Loop Drain-Back Systems

In these systems, when a pump is turned on, solar fluid (distilled water) from a reservoir (drain-back tank, usually 10-gallon) is pushed through the flat-plate or evacuated tube collector and heat exchanger. When the pump is off, the solar fluid drains back into the reservoir. The collector is empty when the pump is off. A high-speed pump feeds the collector and a differential temperature control turns it on and off. Various methods are used to transfer heat from the drain-back tank to the solar storage tank.

The disadvantages of this system are that the collector must be located higher than the reservoir, and drain-back tanks are small and do not store much heat. Drain-back systems are best used in warm climates.

CHAPTER 6
Leaving the Grid: Waste

This chapter is largely a discussion of how to handle human waste in your off-grid lifestyle. But sewage isn't your only waste management problem. Waste of any kind has to be dealt with, and for those wanting to go off-grid, there are some simple solutions to some, but not all, of your waste issues. The key to solid waste management is to generate less solid waste. It doesn't mean buy or eat less—but it does mean waste less. For instance, reuse those bags, receptacles, and containers, as well as any other items that can be used again. Green-minded folks can help by recycling. Off-gridders can go even further and compost much of their solid waste.

Recycling

Recycling is the use of waste material to make a new product. The process consists of collection of recyclables, processing the materials, and manufacturing the product. Among the materials that can be recycled are glass, aluminum cans, steel and other scrap metals, plastic bottles, paper, used motor oil, and old car batteries. The collection and processing steps can be significantly different for each material.

Composting is another form of recycling. It occurs when organic waste is broken down by microbial processes. When the process occurs on the forest floor, it's called mulching and the product is called mulch. When the process is deliberately carried out by people, it's called composting and the product is called compost. The resulting material can be used as fertilizer.

Composting requires water, air, and rotting material with acceptable nitrogen-to-carbon ratio. A composting chamber needs to be durable, with holes for air circulation and a cover to keep out precipitation. Some composter containers are mounted on an axle so they can be rotated to mix the contents. Other containers can be rolled on the ground, or the contents can be mixed with a shovel.

Efficient composting requires careful sorting and mixing of proper ingredients. Compost needs a good supply of nitrogen-rich vegetable waste (called *greens*), which includes scraps from the kitchen and grass and weed clippings. It needs a nearly equal supply of carbon-rich materials (called *browns*), which includes hay, bark, wood chips, dry leaves, shredded paper, or cardboard.

A composter made from a 33-gallon garbage can. Large holes are screened, and there are many tiny holes drilled or poked into it as well. Shock cords keep the lid on tight. To mix the contents the container is tipped and rolled every couple of days. Cost: $16.

Compost radiates heat if the nitrogen/carbon ratio is good. The warmth indicates that aerobic bacteria, worms, and fungi are doing their job. When the process is nearly complete and the compost is ready to be used as fertilizer, the compost will be cool.

Keep an eye on air and moisture levels. The micro-organisms need air to work their magic, so be sure to mix it up and include some wood chips or hay to prevent vegetable products from clumping and to keep the ventilation process going. The mixture should be damp, but not wet enough to drip from the bottom.

The end result is a light, soil-like material called humus—a highly nutritious topsoil that can be spread over vegetable gardens, lawns, fields, and around trees.

Sewage

Domestic wastewater is made up of gray water and black water. *Gray water* comes from the laundry, bathroom sink, kitchen, and appliances—essentially any wastewater not contaminated by feces. *Black water* comes from the toilet and is usually referred to as sewage. Black water is highly pathogenic, but gray water not as much so. Black water must be purified and treated before being reused. Gray water also carries germs and pollutants, but with some precautions it can be reused to water gardens and landscapes. The health departments in some states include gray water from some sources in their definition of black water. Gray water is dirtier than tap water, but generally cleaner than black water. Filtered gray water is most suitably used for sub-surface irrigation of nonedible landscape plants.

Gray-water systems vary from simple, low-cost to highly complex and expensive. All gray-water systems rely on two ideas: First, that healthy topsoil can purify or filter gray water. Second, that humans cannot use gray water for drinking, cooking, or bathing before it is puri-fied. A common (but illegal in most states) method for reusing gray water is to drain it or dump it from buckets directly onto outside vegetation. Sophisticated systems treat gray water prior to disposal using in-line filters or settling tanks and sand filters in order to remove pollut-ants and pathogens before distributing it through a drip system.

Your gray-water system will be based on site, cli-mate, budget, how much gray water you have, how much irrigation you need, soil permeability, how much work you're willing to do, and the local health and build-ing codes. Generally speaking, health departments hate gray-water systems. Bear in mind that water run to draw heated water is not gray water and doesn't need to be treated. Let it flow into a container and then use it to water edible plants.

For most people, gray water is easiest to handle within a septic system. Separate black- and gray-water systems are easy to install during new construction, but to retrofit an older dwelling to handle separate systems is difficult and expensive.

Septic Systems

Let's start with the bottom line here: If you really want an off-grid system of black- and gray-water waste management without coming to blows with the local HD and without having to deal with the maintenance required to work with compost toilets and such, the best option is to install a septic system. As with most of the off-grid preparation we've talked about in this book, you would be very wise to consult an experienced septic system expert to help you, or to install your septic system for you.

A septic system is a large tank, initially filled with water, that collects and releases wastewater. The bacteria in the tank breaks it all down and separates the mess into a middle liquid layer called effluent, sandwiched between a top scum layer of grease, oil, and lighter fluids, and a bottom sludge layer of heavy solids.

When new wastewater flows in, the effluent in the tank flows out into a drain field. The sediment in the drain field acts as a filter, keeping pathogens underground until they're absorbed as soil nutrients. Meanwhile, anaerobic bacteria and other helpful microorganisms feed on the solids in the sludge and scum, breaking it down and creating carbon dioxide and hydrogen sulfide gases that exit through the vent stack.

A septic tank should be emptied and serviced by a professional no less than every three years, and preferably every year. Accumulated solids and scum can eventually fill the tank, clog the system, and contaminate the drain field.

That's the top of the line. Now let's look at the bottom of the line and everything in between. Your local HD will have a heyday with the information you're about to get here.

Composting Toilets

A composting toilet is a warmed, well-ventilated container with diverse microbes that break down and create a dry, fluffy, and odorless compost. This is done with rapid aerobic decomposition, the opposite of anaerobic processes in smelly outhouses. Over 90 percent of the material going into the compost disappears up the vent as a gas or water vapor. A smelly composting toilet means that there are pockets of anaerobic activity caused by inadequate mixing. Below 50° F, microbes stop working or become inactive, and composting stops.

Composting toilets consist of:

- a place to sit;
- a composting chamber; and
- an evaporation tray.

These elements can be combined in a single appliance or appear as separated elements.

In order for composting to work, the chamber needs to be damp. Excess water evaporates in the toilet, and overflow can be plumbed to a septic system. Every composting toilet has a vertical vent pipe to carry off the moisture. Air flows across the evaporation tray and up the vent. The updraft is fueled by the heat of the composting. Electric composters include vent fans and small heating elements to assist with this process. Small composters usually have a mixing device to ensure that oxygen gets to all areas of the pile.

Simple composters use a low-temperature decomposition process known as moldering. They have air channels and fan-driven vents but lack supplemental heat or mixing. Urine and water are usually limited, or not allowed. Liquids must be manually removed or pumped out. The moldering process takes place over years and there is increased pathogen survival.

There are many commercial composting toilets on the market, and the Internet is loaded with ideas for homebuilt composting toilets (type "do-it-yourself composting toilet" into your search engine).

Keeping Your Composter Happy

Anything that adds warmth or increases ventilation will help your composting toilet do its job. Avoid letting a composter compete with other oxygen-using appliances, such as woodstoves. If the composter does not get the oxygen it needs, it will stink. Insulate the vent where it passes through cold spaces so that moisture does not condense and run back down the vent. Every couple of days, add a cup of carbonaceous bulking agent (such as peat or wood chips) to soak up the excess moisture and create air spaces that prevent anaerobic pockets.

Primitive Disposal Systems

Without using a traditional toilet in a septic system or a composting toilet, there are not many health department–approved ways to dispose of human waste. In any case, latrines and toilets are needed to ensure the safe collection of human waste.

Here are the basics of primitive toilets and latrines:

- Provide barriers of privacy of any sort, if possible.
- Locate toilets or latrines away from food-preparation or eating areas.
- Locate toilets and latrines at least 100 feet from bodies of surface water (rivers, lakes, reservoirs, etc.) and at least 100 feet downstream from drinking water sources and habitations.

- Provide running water, if possible, along with toilet paper, soap, paper towels, and garbage disposal next to the toilet. If that's not possible, make hand sanitizer available. Encourage, by whatever means, hand-washing or sanitizing to prevent the spread of severe gastrointestinal diseases. If the toilet or latrine has a door or covers of any kind, keep them closed when not in use to minimize odor and the attraction of insects and animals.
- Consider using camp Porta-potties.

Transient Toilets

River guides and a handful of other outdoorists will recognize this method of human waste disposal. Although the thought of such a system makes us turn up our noses, it's actually much simpler and far less messy or hazardous than one would think.

Line the inside of a 5-gallon bucket or an old toilet bowl with two heavy-duty plastic garbage bags. Secure the excess bag by rolling it up and getting it out of the way so nobody trips on it and dumps the bucket by accident.

It helps to have a seat for the toilet. Some sporting goods stores sell a plastic seat that fits a bucket, but they're a bit flimsy. A cheap hardware store toilet seat can be modified to securely sit on the bucket by epoxying a couple of guideposts to the underside of the seat. Once the garbage bags have been placed to line the bucket, secure the seat to it.

Once daily, add a cup of 1:10 bleach (3 to 6 percent sodium hypochlorite) and water to control pathogens and odor. Or, sprinkle some quicklime (calcium oxide) or a generous amount (a half-cup or so) of kitty litter, ashes, sawdust, or sand over the feces after each use. If you have a limited amount of kitty litter, mix with a filler first (i.e., ashes, sand, or sawdust). There are some commercial chemicals available from sporting goods and RV supply shops, but bleach, quicklime, or kitty litter do just fine and are far less expensive. These precautions reduce bacterial growth and retard the production of methane gas. Used toilet paper and feminine hygiene products can be placed in the toilet.

After each use, it's a good idea to cover the toilet with a big garbage bag to keep the flies out. Keep some hygiene supplies nearby. The minimum should be a bottle of hand sanitizer. Even better would be another 5-gallon bucket full of clean water and a bar of soap. Change the water every day or two.

Barring any disastrous bucket spills, this setup can take care of the potty needs of two people for as long as a month, although the splash factor starts to be a major concern at some point. At the end of the cycle, put on some rubber gloves and squeeze the excess air out of the bags and seal the package by tying the bags off. Store them in a protected area such as inside another bucket with a lid, out of the sun, where animals and insects will not disturb them and the smell will not pervade living and dining areas. Wash your hands when you're finished setting the toilet up again.

So what do you do with that waste? You can't just throw it into the nearest garbage can or Dumpster. It needs to be taken to an approved sanitary landfill, a dumping station, portable john, camp outhouse, or any other site that won't be either unethical or illegal. Most of these depositories are not made to handle plastic or non-sewage waste, so don't just toss the bag in. Wear some disposable gloves and hold the bag over the hole. Use a pair of scissors (kept expressly for that purpose) to cut the corner of the bag. Let as much run out as possible, then squeeze the rest out like a tube of toothpaste. As a courtesy to the garbage collector, put the emptied bag into another clean garbage bag and tie it off before disposing of it in a Dumpster. Wash your hands and the scissors.

Latrines

A latrine is basically a hole that is dug to collect human waste. These can range from "cat holes" (a simple, one-use hole) to large pit and trench latrines for public use. Since it is difficult to know where the hardpan or water table is without digging into it, latrines are not appropriate for urban locations that will continue to be areas of habitation or commerce. The carryover hygiene problems will be unpleasant.

Here are the latrine basics:

- Public-use latrines should be at least 3 feet deep but at least 1 foot above the hardpan or the water table.

- After each use, the "doodie" should be covered with dirt, lime, or ash to keep the odor down and to minimize infestation by insects and animals.

- Consider covering the latrine within a piece of scrap board between uses.

CHAPTER 7
Free Rides and Piggybacking
Off the Grid

Not everyone who gets off the grid does so for altruistic reasons. In fact, most people in Third World countries are off-grid because they have a very limited grid to work with—at least, in terms of what North Americans would understand. Just as interesting is the large group of people in America who essentially live off-grid in such a way that they are not financially responsible for the portion of grid resources they do consume, nor responsible in any way to provide grid resources for others to use. In this world, it is possible to directly or indirectly use unlimited grid resources without lifting a finger to pay for it in the traditional sense. Who are these people? How does this all work out?

First, let's divide these people into some subcultures. The first is a *welfare subculture*—those whose consumption of grid resources outweighs their production of resources simply because of their inability to support themselves financially. If they had the money, most of them would love to have the choice to live off- or on-grid and pay for or produce their share, but for the moment their present circumstances do not allow them any choice. The result is that they reap the benefits of the grid without having the responsibility to contribute to or pay for it. The expense is borne by tax-payers and by donations and grants. We—you and I—feed, shelter, and provide waste management for these people.

The second is a *vagabond subculture*. People in this group are most often, though not always, quite capable of producing grid resources, but are simply not interested. They may hunker down in a commune or collective farm, or may wander the countryside and the world living as cheaply as possible and taking advantage (in a rational and respectable sense) of the grid resources easily available to them.

The third is a *career subculture*. Their professional or volunteer careers, their politics, or their crimes place them directly under the care of an agency or organization that is fully responsible for the grid resources they consume. In many cases the agencies and organizations, as well as the individual members of this group, turn a blind eye to the resources they burn, and often burn them in enormously disproportionate amounts.

Grid resources—shelter, and the power to cook, clean, and handle waste management—are provided for the welfare subculture in three forms: food provision (food banks and soup kitchens), shelter (shantytowns, flophouses, and goodwill shelters), and miscellaneous (subsidies of various kinds).

In the vagabond subculture, grid resources are often provided by friends and neighbors who invite an individual or group to join them in their homes, collective farms, or communal sites. These individuals or groups are commonly asked to take some small part of the responsibility for off-grid resources. Communal sites are often excellent producers of off-grid resources

A treehouse at a communal site on Maui. Individuals accepted onto the land can build dwellings and grow gardens on small jungle sites in return for a commitment to stay and just one hour of work per day to contribute to the community survival and financial needs.

that result from the sum of individual efforts within the group.

Vagabonding may also fall under the squatting category. *Squatting* is normally a derogatory term, but here we're using it simply as a category into which we can place the use of fee-free living space and its associated grid resources. There are a lot of very interesting lifestyles that fit into this category; for example, those who use free campground space (e.g., abandoned building sites, Bureau of Land Management lands). Let's also include expeditionary adventuring (essentially, outdoor adventure trips into the backcountry or remote areas that last two weeks or more) as part of this category. Some groups—for example, mountain climbing expeditions—go for months in the backcountry or into Third World locations, carrying along with them their own "mini-grid." This can be very expensive, but a surprisingly large number of people are able to perpetuate this lifestyle by providing promotional material to their corporate sponsors. Free shelter, free food, free fuel, free gear, free fun for as long as the members of the team can make their sponsors happy.

Finally, vagabonding often falls under the *clubbing* category. This is where the vagabond pays bargain rates for austere living conditions that include access to grid resources. The vagabond himself is not responsible for anything to do with the grid. These include private hospitality clubs and places like the YMCA.

Another potential addition to this list would be the eternal student . . . living on or off campus with Mom and Dad's money, casually changing majors and pursuing questionable social goals.

The career subculture of grid avoiders includes military personnel under the watchful care of Uncle Sam, and commercial sailors and offshore oil riggers whose grids are right there with them on the boat or oil rig. It would also include employees in any remote permanent station where the staff lives independently from major utility resources. Grid ignorance is often one of the perks enjoyed by many government workers and politicians,

Campground host's solar rig, courtesy of the U.S. government.

and it's certainly an inherent part of the life led by criminals in prison (please excuse the use of the words *politicians* and *criminals* in the same sentence).

The career subculture also includes those groups and individuals who accept a reduced reliance on the grid as a normal part of their service, including VISTA and Peace Corps volunteers, missionaries, backcountry rangers, and campground hosts, among others.

So what is the purpose of this chapter? It's simply to acknowledge that all off-grid lifestyles are not voluntary or a result of noble sacrifice on anyone's part. For many people the problem with the grid is the fact that one has to pay for it, and for many of those individuals, the answer is to make someone else pay for it, or to simply do without.

Here are some websites of interest:

- *A list of shelters and soup kitchens in the United States*: http://4homeless.hypermart.net/soup_kitchens.html

- *A network of people around the world who offer free accommodations, advice, and help for travelers*: http://www.hospitalityclub.org/

CHAPTER 8
Communicating and Making
a Living Off-Grid

Distant communication is seldom discussed in regard to off-grid living, even though a remote off-gridder can communicate over long distances without hardwiring into the communications grid. But there's a conundrum: Just because your Internet service provider (ISP) is wireless doesn't mean you're off the grid. In fact, you are absolutely, without doubt, totally dependent on the communications grid—the series of towers and transmitters and cables and satellites that exemplify today's technology. Wireless does *not* mean off-grid. You may get your power from your PV array, but in order to communicate data, you are otherwise tied to the grid. Now that *that* bubble has been burst . . .

Telephone Communication
Landlines

POTS (Plain Old Telephone Systems) are tied together through above- or below-ground hardwired networks. These traditional systems are powered through the phone line and will work even if your battery bank is out of service, as long as the POTS lines and stations are functioning. Portable phones (not to be mistaken for cell phones) need house electricity to charge and function.

Cell Phones

Cell phones rely on radio waves between the phone and cellular towers. They can be charged in your car, on house current, or even by crank chargers.

Satellite Phones

Satellite phones transmit through low-orbiting satellites. They don't work indoors without a satellite dish, and they are heavy and expensive. Under the current circumstances, it would be cheaper to pay for satellite Internet service and rely on any of several computer telephone services, such as Skype or Yahoo!'s Phone Out and Phone In. Sadly, a problem with using voice over Internet phone (VoIP) services through a satellite is the likelihood of problems with latency. Latency, also known as "ping time" is basically the round-trip time of the data to the satellite and back.

Radio

Of all the resources available, simple radio is about as off-grid as modern communications can possibly be. In the United States radio communications are regulated by the Federal Communications Commission, which assigns radio frequencies according to function. Radio signals, like all electromagnetic radiation, travel in straight lines. However, at low frequencies (LF, below 3 MHz), diffraction effects allow them to partially follow the earth's curvature, thus allowing AM radio signals in low-noise environments to be heard well after the transmitting antenna has dropped below the horizon. Additionally, frequencies between approximately 3 and 30 MHz (HF, or high frequency), can be reflected by the ionosphere, thus giving radio transmissions in this frequency range a potentially global reach.

At higher frequencies (very high and ultra-high frequencies, or VHF and UHF), none of these effects apply, and any obstruction between the transmitting and receiving antenna will block the signal. The ability to visually sight a transmitting antenna roughly corresponds with the ability to receive a signal from it. This propagation characteristic of high-frequency radio is called "line-of-sight." Line-of-sight is a limitation for any high-frequency radio system, including cell and Wireless Internet Service Providers (see below).

In practice, the propagation characteristics of these radio bands vary substantially depending on the exact frequency and the strength of the transmitted signal (a function of both transmitter power and antenna characteristics).

Low-powered transmitters, like the Family Radio Service (FRS) and General Mobile Radio Service (GMRS) radios you get at the local discount store, can be blocked by a few trees, buildings, hills, or even heavy rain or snow. The presence of nearby objects not in the direct line of sight can also interfere with radio transmission. Reflected radiation from the ground plane also acts to cancel out the direct signal. This effect can be reduced by raising the antenna further from the ground. The reduction in signal loss is known as height gain, and it's the reason large mobile and base antennas get better propagation than hand radios running the same wattage.

FRS, Multi-Use Radio Service (MURS), and Citizens Band (CB) do not require licensing. GMRS does require a license, so if you're using a GMRS/FRS combination radio, you'll need the license. GMRS and CB do not require an examination. In all countries amateur radio (known as ham radio) licensing requires an examination to prove knowledge of basic radio electronics and communications rules and regulations. In return, hams get more frequencies (larger "bands") and can use a much wider variety of communications technologies at substantially higher power. For ham licensing information go to www.arrl.org. For all U.S. licensing and regulations information, go to www.fcc .gov/licensing.html or www.arrl.org. Get information for

Canadian licensing at http://www.rac.ca/regulatory/
liceinfo.htm

Wireless Internet Service Providers (WISPs)

WISPs provide wireless high-speed Internet access for
computers, cell phones, and other handheld devices at
speeds comparable to hardwired cable and DSL. This
allows the user to do e-mail and text messaging, and to
download large file formats such as streaming media.
Almost every laptop and many handheld devices on
today's market have factory-installed wireless modems.

All that's required for a laptop computer to be WISP-
capable is a compatible operating system (Windows 98,
XP, or Vista, for example), an Ethernet card, or a USB/
Ethernet adaptor compatible with the specific ISP you're
going to use. Today's mobile computing devices (such
as smartphones and PDAs) will have WISP-capability
already on board.

This would be a good place to mention that the
household or office wireless local area network (LAN)
system is *not* the same as a WISP. Household LANs are
based on a hardwired device that transmits broadband
access to other devices within the LAN. It's like the
difference between a cell phone and portable phone.
You can use the cell phone anywhere within the tower

range, but the portable phone only works within the transmitting range of the primary telephone base. Try taking it out of the house and it won't work.

It's important for budding off-gridders to understand that WISP services are not available everywhere. WISPs use a tower transmitting system similar to that of cell phone service providers. If you don't live within the tower's range, you don't get service. Like the cell system, there are nationwide and global WISPs that concentrate on putting their tower systems (hot spots) where they will serve the greatest number of people (T-Mobile, Clearwire). Local WISPs cover smaller, specific regions (towns). If you live in the boonies, many times you're just out of luck. But all is not lost. For a few dollars more, there's satellite Internet service.

Satellite Internet service has definite advantages: generally excellent and reliable service and fewer of the types of outages experienced on the WISPs or hardwired services. Service is available anywhere in the United States at locations that have an unobstructed southern sky. The initial investment will be for installation of a small satellite dish and the indoor transceiver system. The monthly charges will run roughly twice that of the WISPs.

Off-grid wireless is a fantasy. Modern communication requires a grid, whether it's hardwired or wireless. Until wireless and satellite Internet service is cheaper than DSL and other hardwired broadband services, why not just accept that it's okay to have a cable running into your house or office?

Making Your Living Off-Grid

If you're a truck driver you're essentially already making an off-grid living, with the exception that the road itself is a grid, and everything you purchase en route comes from the grid. Surprisingly, though, truckers who spend a lot of time on the road use a lot of DC power or AC inverter power to get them through the day or night. Stop at any big truck stop and take a look at the DC appliances available on the shelves: inverters, radios, toaster ovens, electric blankets, coffeemakers, cooler-refrigerators, solar panels, televisions, and water heaters—not to mention the plug-ins for computers, cell phones, and spotlights. Intentional or not, these folks make their livings off the traditional grid, and they've got the technology to show for it.

So, in reality, what we are talking about when we say "making a living off-grid" is what everyone else calls "work-at-home jobs." With high-speed Internet access available almost anywhere, there are some good-paying choices for people who want the flexibility of a career that doesn't require a trip to the office every day. These kinds of jobs are perfect for off-gridders who enjoy their privacy and freedom.

The problem is that finding profitable off-grid work that is legitimate isn't easy. In the movies we've all seen the exaggerated trailer-trash examples of traveling flea-market businesses. That sort of enterprise does indeed exist, and the stereotypical characters seen in those depictions seem to be fairly accurate. If that lifestyle is not your cup of tea, here are a few other options to try:

Be a Call Center

No, you do not have to move to India or Pakistan for this. Call-routing technology has evolved significantly and companies are finding that they can outsource order taking, sales, and problem-solving calls to home-based workers. According to some reports, home-based workers tend to be more highly educated and more loyal to their employer than their equals at traditional outsourced call centers.

Typically a home-based operator is a contractor who is paid for each minute spent on the phone. That way companies are not paying for off-phone time, and the employee can guiltlessly go on with his or her life until the phone rings again or it's time to make another call. The problem with call-centering is the low pay usually starting at between $7 and $8 per hour at the time of this writing. Order-taking and phone survey jobs generally pay the least. Sales jobs pay more but are definitely harder. Ideally you'll find a call-center job that requires some technical expertise with computer hardware or software. These jobs require paid training and can result in a certification that you can use later to land another job or build a résumé.

Two final points: First, you will need a dedicated phone line, a computer, and high-speed Internet. Second, call centers cannot tolerate serious distractions. Barking dogs, crying babies, or blaring TVs and stereos can get you fired.

Do Business on the Web

We're talking about eBay and its copycats. A lot of people make money at this. Many look for bargains at local retailers and then auction the booty off for a profit. Auction sites have tutorials to help beginners get started. Take some time and do some research. Remember that your reputation is going to be the key to good sales. Be organized, describe your items honestly, and ship items immediately to ensure your reputation is impeccable.

Auction site business is not cost-free. You'll be paying listing costs, the site's commissions, and you'll have a few buyers that won't pay you. Plan on getting started slowly, and don't invest in a lot of garbage you might not be able to sell.

Other Ideas

Some other ideas for at-home or off-grid business might include mystery shopping (where you're paid to pose as a customer to critique store service), survey-taking, audiotape transcription, inventory-taking, and the like. This kind of piecemeal work can be hard to find and the pay is usually downright unacceptable. But in a pinch, it can get you by.

There are certainly other home-based businesses that can be attempted: child care, house-sitting, dog-walking, errand running, virtual assisting, etc. Use classified ads and the Internet to connect with customers. Don't be afraid to post a few handouts around town. Make sure you know your community's licensure and insurance requirements. Take time to draft a business plan (see http://www.sba.gov/smallbusinessplanner/index.html).

Of course, there are those who are wealthy and well-established enough that they can simply operate their megabusinesses from their home by telephone and computer. These folks already know who they are, and need no advice from this book.

Finally, if all else fails, become a cowboy or a sheepherder. There's no grid on the open range. Yippy-ai-kai-yay.

For the rest of us, if we want to delve into making our livings in our off-grid surroundings, here are some words of wisdom:

- Don't expect to make millions.
- Do expect plenty of competition.
- Don't get scammed. If it seems too good to be true, it's not true.
- First, try to make your current job portable. Your employer might just go for it.

CHAPTER 9
Living the Life: Case Studies

From the moment I first outlined the notes for this book, I planned to fill the final chapter with success stories about off-grid living—and there are plenty of them. What I've found as I've spoken with off-gridders is that each one of them is proud of what they've done, and each of them has at least one annoying glitch in whatever system they've created. A perfect off-grid life is impossible, just as a perfect on-grid life is.

Let's take a glimpse at a handful of off-grid stories. We'll avoid the rich-folks-go-green stories because they simply consist of the wealthy shelling out enough money for somebody else to turn their property into an off-grid showpiece. Boring.

Case 1: Rancho Margot, Costa Rica

I was a guest at Rancho Margot for a week, serving as a first-aid instructor for their adventure guides. The ranch is owned by the Sostheim family and is truly a great example of a successful attempt to develop a self-sustaining community.

Rancho Margot sits on 40 acres near the shores of Lake Arenal, beneath a volcano and in the valley of the Cano Negro River. It is splendidly covered with primary rain forest and has eleven natural springs. The Sostheim family wants to preserve the area as much as possible, and Rancho Margot is the ranger station for the Children's Eternal Rain Forest.

The ranch is run as a quiet, remote tourist destination with guest facilities and adventure programs. Most of the work on the ranch is done by volunteer resident help, and accommodations and meals are exchanged for skills and work.

A large part of the building materials used at Margot came directly from the forest and riverway. Power is generated with a Pelton-wheel micro-hydro system, and waste is either composted or sent to septic systems. Biogas is made from pig manure and used for heating and other purposes (see the appendices in the back of the book for an introduction to biogas).

Milk and dairy products are processed on-site. Poultry and beef are raised and processed on the ranch. Fish is available from the lake. A large vegetable garden provides produce, and there's also a medicinal garden. The bar/restaurant, communal dining facilities, and kitchen are located within a few yards of the stable. With animal diet control and good hygienic procedures by the stable staff, there is virtually no smell or fly problem.

They are feeling some growing pains, and transportation to and from the ranch is as grid-tied as transportation anywhere else. But this is an exceptional place to get a taste of what can be done off-grid, and how self-sustainability can be done with style.

Case 2: Eric

Eric would probably be called a vagrant by most people, but to the folks in Blanding, Utah, he was just Eric. A large, strong-framed black man of fifty-seven, Eric had put down roots, so to speak, in the quiet Mormon town near the Four Corners area. He lived across the street from Blanding's only grocery store, in a vacant lot, no roof over his head, and with no possessions except a few books and the sorts of personal items that could fit into the pockets of his pants.

As for the grid, there was none. Eric lived in the dirt and weeds of the near-empty lot. He couldn't have chosen a more unlikely place to call home. A non-Mormon black man squatting in the city limits was unusual to say the least. But somehow Eric made friends and blended in. He became popular with the young people, especially with the teenage Navajo youth that lived nearby.

Eric kept to himself and behaved like a gentleman. He was shy, studious, and intelligent. Nobody got robbed or mugged as they walked by. Nobody's child went missing. There were no drunken brawls. Within a week or so the town essentially adopted Eric, and he was bombarded with gifts of clothing, food, water, blankets, sleeping bags, tents, and chairs. Most often he would turn them down with a polite thank-you. Sometimes he would take the gift and wait until the giver was out of sight, then place the gift in the dumpster. Eric didn't want much. He had the sun and the stars, and except for an occasional cool drink of water and an occasional visit to a clean restroom, he didn't have much use for the grid. For entertainment he would read, and to keep in shape he lifted the boulders that were strewn around the lot. If he needed protection from the rain or sun, he crawled beneath a tilted flatbed trailer that the owner had offered as shelter. He wasn't social, but people liked him and waved cheerfully as they drove by.

This is an example of a man so far off the grid that any of our own efforts to become self-sustaining pale in comparison.

As he became familiar with the lot that the town seemed to have deeded to him, he developed an interest in agriculture. Some of those few he would speak to remembered that he talked about coming back to Blanding in the spring to plant a garden.

Winters in Blanding are harsh. At 6,000 feet it gets cold and snowy. The local law enforcement offered to drive him 300 miles to a warm resort town near the

Nevada border where temperatures were comfortable. Eric turned the offer down, and decided instead to go to Page, Arizona, for a few months. Page is a couple of thousand feet lower, and so a good 10 degrees warmer. He would go there, pass time through the winter, and return to Blanding to plant his garden.

A week after his arrival in Page, Eric, the "gentle eccentric," was beaten to death in a well-lit area of Page's main park. Being off-grid is different, and some people just can't stand difference.

Case 3: Maui, North Coast

A few miles east of Kahului, Maui, is a popular pullout where tourists can buy fruit and handicrafts and wander up a number of trails to see some great waterfall scenery. What they don't see in the tropical forest above them is a 40-acre community of some thirty to sixty people. The owners are stewards of the incredible landscape and keep it open to the public. Like many of the residents of Rancho Margot, those living here are trading their skills for a place in paradise. Here the group expects an hour of work per day per person on communal projects, and in exchange the participant is invited onto a small parcel of land where he or she can build a small shelter. Those who stay long-term usually build a more-sophisticated alternative structure. Most residents live completely off-grid, many of them with no electricity or running water.

Water is carried from a nearby mountain stream. Other residents have built magnificent yurt-like round houses, supplied with PV electricity and hot water from solar collectors (many of the photos used in the book were taken at this location). Waste is composted. There are community and individual gardens, and some residents keep poultry and other small farm animals. Many fish the local stream for prawns and crawfish, and scavenge the abundant natural fruit in the forest. The group gets capital from sales to tourists. It doesn't get much more kicked-back than this.

Case 4: Clark Farm, Burley, Idaho

After all the complicated material you've read in this book, it's time to put it to rest with something simple: the Clark farm in Burley, Idaho. This could be any old farmhouse in virtually any part of the country, and the reason I mention it here is because it's a reminder of the way life used to be. Going off-grid is nothing new; it's just a revitalization of old lifestyles. The Clarks grew up during the Depression, and like most survivors of that era, they learned to fend for themselves, make do with what they had, and help their neighbors.

The wood-frame 1,300-square-foot house is probably eighty or ninety years old. The Clarks have owned it for forty-two of those years. Back when it was built there was no electric utility in that part of town, so it had to be retrofitted for wiring. Electricity is essentially the only part of the classic grid that serves the home. All water needs are satisfied by a well. Electric pumps are backed up with hand pumps in case there's a power outage. Black- and gray water go into a septic system that has been functioning without problems since the house was built. Heat is provided by a wood-burning stove. Cooling is managed by taking advantage of evapotranspiration and shade from a densely planted flower garden and big trees that surround the home. Thick insulation and double-paned storm windows help, and the house stays cozy year-round. Under the house is an old-style "root cellar" where produce can be stored at 50° F (a refrigerator or freezer located in the cellar works less and saves substantial energy.) The Clarks don't have a garbage service, so they compost whatever they can and haul the rest to the dump.

Once upon a time, this is how it was for nearly everyone in America. Now some of us, for whatever reason, are looking to get back to that lifestyle.

Appendix 1
Off-Grid Venue Comparison

Generalized Off-Grid Venue Comparison

Transient or Mobile

RV's, boats, tents, emergency shelters, homes with <250 square feet floor space.

Intermittent

Small homes, partial homes or sections of structures, vacation cabins, seasonal habitations with <750 square feet of floor space.

Permanent

Large homes and businesses.

Power production & distribution

Transient or Mobile

For solar, this will typically require at least one 15–18 watt panel and one high capacity deep-cycle battery.

A **stand-alone** DC system will usually consist of a solar array, charge controller, battery bank, and a load center. A load center might consist of meters and fuses, or fuses may exist between the battery bank and the controller, and between the controller and the load.

The advantage of a stand-alone DC system is that there is no inverter to fail.

Stand-alone DC-AC systems are basically the same but include an inverter to change DC to AC. Usually an inexpensive square wave or modified square wave inverter is enough. Fluorescent lights may not turn on with a cheap load-demand inverter.

Transmission of low volt DC over long distances requires large-guage wire.

Intermittent

Stand alone DC-AC systems use AC to run common low-power household appliances.

If the structure is already wall-wired for utility power, consider transient wiring outside the wall with a multiple-outlet extension cord.

Keep a generator and battery charger on hand in case the system fails.

A stand-alone AC system commonly consists of ten or more solar panels, a very large battery bank, and one or more inverters. Some inverters can be wired in series or parallel to produce 240 volts, to boost amperage, or to provide a backup in case one inverter fails.

The inverter(s) will probably be modified square wave types. A stand-alone AC system can use standard wiring, switches, outlets, and fixtures.

A hybrid system is a good idea if you want to avoid gigantic solar arrays and huge battery banks.A hybrid system often consists of a combination of solar and microhydro, wind, and generator (gas, propane, or diesel). During cloudy periods or when the load demand is high, the generator can be started. The generator or other turbines (wind, microhydro) can be used to power AC loads and to recharge low batteries.

Permanent

In a **utility interface** system the grid is connected but the PV, wind, or microhydro systems provide much of the power. If the batteries are low, an auto transfer switch connects to the grid until the battery banks have been recharged. The switch then reconnects to the inverter. A utility interface is cheaper than an intertie.

Some people use a modified sine wave inverter for daily work loads and a small sine wave inverter for electronics.

Utility intertie systems. Instead of storing extra power in batteries, it is sold to the utility company. These systems use a sine wave inverter to change DC to low-distortion AC. Power is delivered to the gird through a kilowatt-hour meter as it is produced. A second meter measures any grid power consumed at the home.

The disadvantage of an intertie system is that there's no real power storage, and if the grid fails, there's no backup. Keep a generator around for emergencies.

Lighting

Transient or Mobile

In small or mobile habitations low voltage DC is best. It can be transmitted short distances over narrow gauge wire.

Low volt fluorescent bulbs have three to four times the light output per watt than incandescent bulbs. Halogen is 30 percent more efficient than fluorescent, and seems far brighter.

In a large multi-light habitation, use an inverter but keep a few DC lights on hand in case the inverter fails.

AC light dimmers may not work without a pure sine wave inverter.

Also, fluorescent lights may not turn on with a load demand inverter.

Intermittent

AC fluorescent lighting is the common choice.

Permanent

AC fluorescent lighting is the common choice.

Space heating and cooling

Transient or Mobile

To warm a cold RV or tent takes about 1000 BTU's per 50 square feet of floor space.

A catalytic heater burns without flames, so it produces less carbon monoxide.

Intermittent

Passive solar design goes a long way toward off-grid heating and cooling.

Propane and wood are the cheapest and most easily obtainable fuel for space heating.

Appliances with motors (e.g. air conditioners, swamp coolers, heater fan, etc) may require an inverter with 2000 or more watts of surge power.

Permanent

Passive solar design goes a long way toward off-grid heating and cooling.

Appliances with motors (e.g. air conditioners, swamp coolers, heater fan, etc) may require an inverter with 2000 or more watts of surge power.

Water heating and distribution

Transient or Mobile

Water sources: springs water or other public access water; catchment systems; transported and kept in containers.

Backpacker-type solar showers are OK for summer use, but have dismal performance in winter, even in full sun.

Single and double burner camp heaters are available for the kitchen and shower. With a single burner the water may be tepid. Cycle it twice to make it hot.

Manually pressurized hot water showers can be purchased or made from a garden pump spray tank.

Add hot water and pump to pressurize. DO NOT ADD BOILING WATER AND DO NOT HEAT THE PUMP CONTAINER.

Intermittent

Water sources: wells, springs, generally via plumbed lines; catchment systems.

Propane, natural gas, solar heaters. Refer to chapter 6.

Permanent

Water sources: wells and springs via plumbed lines.

Propane, natural gas, solar heaters. Refer to chapter 6.

Laundry & cleaning

Transient or Mobile

Portable DC vacuum cleaner (e.g. the Coleman wet/dry vac) are inexpensive.

Hand wash or use a laundromat.

Intermittent

Energy efficient washing machine.

Hang to dry.

Motors for belt-driven AC devices can be replaced with a high-efficiency AC or DC motor.

Permanent

Energy efficient washing machine and dryer (electric or propane).

Standard vacuum cleaners run at 600 to 800 watts.

Standard washing machines run at 800–1000 watts, using 300 to 400 watts per load. Motors for belt-driven AC devices can be replaced with a high-efficiency AC or DC motor.

Refrigeration

Transient or Mobile

Low watt 12V DC cooler/refrigerators. Inexpensive but frequently fail.

A durable high quality DC refrigerator is expensive but saves on the cost of the number of solar panels and batteries required.

Intermittent

Gas-powered absorption refrigerators use bottled LP gas at least 5–10 gallons per month.

Permanent

Energy efficient standard-sized refrigerators and freezers. An AC fridge should be rated at 300 to 400 kWh.

Cooking

Transient or Mobile

Bottled propane stoves are the popular choice in this venue.

Intermittent

LP stoves are common.

Microwave ovens are more efficient than their propane or electric counterparts.

Permanent

LP stoves are common.

Microwave ovens are more efficient than their propane or electric counterparts.

Electronics, tools, small appliances

Transient or Mobile

Stereos, TVs, DVD & CD players, and computers may have low pawer draw. Many are available with both

DC and AC input. The DC models usually use less power.

Intermittent

Small appliances (irons, toasters) use lots of power but are used briefly and infrequently, so as long as the battery and inverter are large enough, they are OK to use.

Permanent

Energy-efficient appliances. Turn off appliances to avoid phantom loads.

Waste management

Transient or Mobile

Latrines, porta-potties, public bathrooms.
    Recycling of non-sewage waste.

Intermittent

Composting or incinerating toilets, or low-water volume flush toilets to a septic system.
    Composting or recycling of non-sewage waste.

Permanent

Low-water volume flush toilets into a septic system.
Composting or recycling of non-sewage waste.

Appendix 2
Resources

Here are some resources to help you with your off-grid planning. Generous use of your search engine will help you locate everything you want to know. To find additional information on the books listed here, go to amazon.com or an online bookstore, or just type the title of the book in your search engine.

Websites
Solar Energy

Basics of Solar Power: http://www.solar4power.com/solar-power-basics.html

Florida Solar Energy Center: http://www.fsec.ucf.edu/en/consumer/

Rocky Mountain Solar: http://www.rockymtsolar.com

Solar Array Tech Guides: http://www.solarray
.com/TechGuides

Solar Energy: http://encyclobeamia.solarbotics
.net/articles

Solar Hot-Water Basics: http://www.homepower
.com/basics/hotwater/

Solar Panels: http://www.ferrispowerproducts
.com/22-29.pdf

Solar Panels: http://www.wholesalesolar.com/
Information-SolarFolder/mount-info.html

**Solar Power Integration/Solar System
Solutions:** http://www.solarexpert.com

Solar and Renewable Energy: http://www
.realgoods.com

Sustainable and Renewable Energy

AC Generator: http://www.ncert.nic.in/html/
learning_basket/electricity/electricity/machine/
ac_generator.htm

altE University (Making Renewable Do-able):
http://howto.altenergystore.com

**Consumer's Guide to Energy Efficiency and
Renewable Energy:** http://www.eere.energy
.gov/consumer/your_home/electricity

Database of State Incentives for Renewables and Efficiency: http://www.dsireusa.org

ENERGY STAR: http://energystar.custhelp.com

Micro-Hydro Power: http://www.microhydropower.com/staffpubs/staff1.htm

Off-Grid and Renewables Tutorial: http://www.green-trust.org/offgridtutor.htm

Power Inverters for Your Truck, Boat, RV, or Alternative Energy System: http://www.donrowe.com

Sustainable Building, Development, and ECO Construction: http://www.sustainablebuild.co.uk

Food, Water, and Waste Management

Dehydrated Foods/Storage: http://waltonfeed.com

How to Build a Septic System: http://www.economic.com/septic.htm

Rainwater Collection System: http://www.wikihow.com/Build-a-Rainwater-Collection-System

Sustainable Harvest International: http://www.sustainableharvest.org

Miscellaneous

FCC Licensing Systems: http://www.fcc.gov/licensing.html

Intentional Communities: http://directory.ic.org/iclist/geo.php

Natural Resources Defense Council: http://www.nrdc.org

Books

The Art of Natural Building by Joseph F. Kennedy, Michael Smith, Catherine Wanek (New Society Publishers, 2002).

Building with Cob: A Step-by-Step Guide by Adam Weismann, Katy Bryce (Green Books, 2006).

Building with Earth: A Guide to Flexible-Form Earthbag Construction (A Real Goods Solar Living Book) by Paulina Wojciechowska (Chelsea Green, 2001).

The Cob Builders Handbook: You Can Hand-Sculpt Your Own Home by Becky Bee (Groundworks, 1998).

The Complete Yurt Handbook by Paul King (Eco-Logic Books, 2002).

Cordwood Building: The State of the Art by Rob Roy (New Society Publishers, 2003).

Design Like You Give a Damn: Architectural Responses to Humanitarian Crises (Architecture for Humanity) by Kate Stohr, Cameron Sinclair (Metropolis Books, 2006).

Earthbag Building: The Tools, Tricks and Techniques (Natural Building Series) by Kaki Hunter, Donald Kiffmeyer (New Society Publishers, 2004).

Earth-Sheltered Houses: How to Build an Affordable Underground Home by Rob Roy (New Society Publishers, 2006).

The Homeowner's Guide to Renewable Energy: Achieving Energy Independence through Solar, Wind, Biomass and Hydropower by Dan Chiras (New Society Publishers, 2006).

The Natural House: A Complete Guide to Healthy, Energy-Efficient, Environmental Homes by Dan Chiras (Chelsea Green, 2000).

The Natural Plaster Book: Earth, Lime, and Gypsum Plasters for Natural Homes by Cedar Rose Guelberth, Dan Chiras (New Society Publishers, 2002).

The Passive Solar House: The Complete Guide to Heating and Cooling Your Home by James Kachadorian (Chelsea Green, 2006).

Real Goods Solar Living Source Book: Your Complete Guide to Renewable Energy Technologies and Sustainable Living by John Schaeffer (Gaiam Real Goods, 2007).

The Solar House: Passive Heating and Cooling by Dan Chiras (Chelsea Green, 2002).

Appendix 3
Power System Diagrams
and Photos

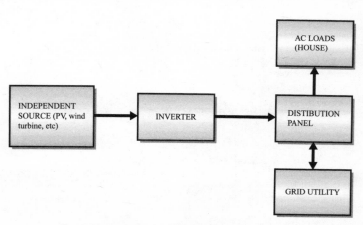

Above, a simplified diagram of a **typical grid-tied power system**. Power systems are either grid-tied (utility-connected; utility interactive, grid-dependent, etc.) or stand-alone. Stand alone systems operate independent of the grid. Utility-connected systems operate in parallel with and interconnected with the local utility company's grid. These grid-tied systems have an independent source (PV array, wind turbine, etc.) that feeds

DC into an inverter to make AC, which is then distributed to AC loads in the house, or if more than is needed is produced, the extra is fed into the grid electric system. If not enough is produced, the grid is tapped to make up the difference.

Below, a **direct-coupled power system**. These usually run a single small DC appliance, such as a pump.

A stand-alone system with battery-bank storage:

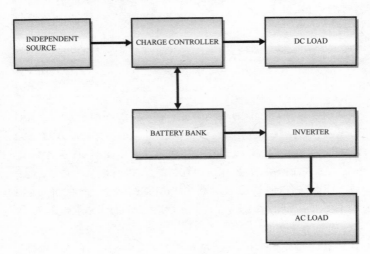

Independent hybrid, backed-up system:

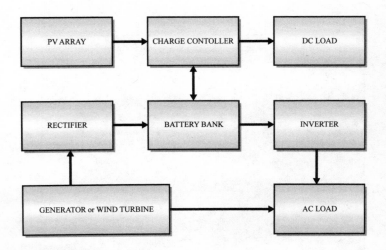

This photo sequence shows a mobile power station used to power the home of a Bureau of Land Management campground host:

Solar array mounted on a trailer. Note the ground wire leading from the system and spiked into the earth near the trailer hitch.

AC and DC disconnects and receptacles, mounted on the rear of the box.

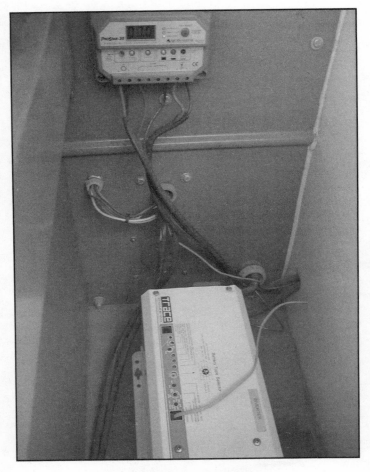

Charge controller (small box) and inverter (large box), mounted inside one of two box compartments. Across from them, in the next compartment, is the battery bank.

Appendix 4
Sizing Your System

Estimating Your Energy Needs

Simply put, a load is any appliance or device that consumes electricity. To figure out your energy needs, and before you can size your charging devices (solar panels, generators, etc.), you need to figure out how much power your loads (appliances) will demand.

Start with your AC loads. Look on the back of your appliance and it will have a label that lists how many watts the appliance consumes. If not, it will probably list the volts and amps it consumes, and then you just apply the simple power formula you learned earlier. That is, power is the product of voltage times amperage:

Power (watts) = E (in volts) × I (in amperes)

If none of this information appears on the back of your appliance, look it up on the Internet.

Now that you know how to find or figure out the watts your appliance uses, make a list of all of the appliances you plan to run in your solar, wind, hydro, generator, or hybrid system. Next to each appliance, list the hours per week you estimate the appliance will be run. For each appliance, multiply watts by hours to get the watt-hours per week you'll be using.

Watt-hours (WH) = watts × hours

Add the watt-hours from each appliance and get the total for your AC appliances, then multiply it by 1.2 to make up for the power loss through your inverter.

Now do the same for your DC loads. Then add the AC and DC watt-hour totals. Divide this number by the voltage of your system (12, 24, 36, or 48V). This tells you how many amp-hours you'll use in a week. Divide by 7 to get your daily amp-hour needs. So, to recap:

Watt-hours per week (WH/wk) = watts × hours/wk.
Figure AC WH/wk. Adjust for inverter power loss.
   Add DC WH/wk.
Amp-hours = WH/system voltage
Daily needs = weekly needs/7

Sizing Your Battery Bank

To greatly simplify the task of sizing your battery bank, let's just say you need enough amp-hours stored in your batteries to last you for three or four cold, cloudy days without dropping your battery charge below 50 percent.

Figure out your daily amp-hour needs, multiply by 3 or 4, then double that. Or to grossly simplify, amp-hours per day needed × 8. You need to have enough batteries to supply that many amp hours. You can get the amp-hours to charge the battery from solar or generator or wind or hydro or a hybrid, but that's how many amp-hours you're going to need if you're off-grid.

Deep-cycle batteries are rated either by reserve capacity in minutes or by amp-hours. Reserve capacity is a measure of how long a battery can deliver a certain amount of current—usually 25 amps. Amp-hour capacity is a measure of how many amps a battery can deliver for a specified length of time—usually 20 or 24 hours. To convert reserve capacity to amp-hour capacity, multiply the reserve capacity by the specified current. In order to determine how many batteries you need, you'll need to already know the amp-hour capacity of the batteries you plan to buy.

Here's a somewhat more exact way to figure out how many batteries you'll need and how they will need to be configured:

Step 1. Figure out the total watt-hours needed daily to run your loads.

Step 2. Multiply the watt-hours from Step 1 by the number of days of power needs you wish to store for (3 or 4).

Step 3. Multiply the number carried from Step 4 by 2 (to ensure batteries don't discharge to less than 50 percent capacity).

Step 4. Estimate the lowest temperature the battery bank will be subjected to, and use the corresponding number to multiply by the figure from Step 3:

80 degrees F	1.00
70	1.04
60	1.11
50	1.19
40	1.30
30	1.40
20	1.50

Step 5. Divide the figure from Step 4 by the system voltage. This will be the amp-hour capacity of your battery bank.

Step 6. By now you should have decided which battery you're going to build your bank with, and you know what its amp-hour capacity is. Divide the figure from Step 5 by the battery's amp-hour capacity. The result is the number of batteries you'll need wired in parallel. Round the figure up to the next higher number (you can't have 5.2 batteries in your bank, but you can have 6).

Step 7. Divide the system voltage by the voltage of the battery you have chosen. This figure will be the number of batteries you'll need wired in series.

The total number of individual batteries you will need to complete your battery bank will be the product of the number of parallel strings needed to meet your amp-hour requirement and the number of batteries per string needed to meet your system voltage requirement.

Total # batteries in bank = (# series strings) × (# batteries per string)

When batteries are cabled together in series, the voltages add together. When batteries are connected in parallel, the voltage remains constant and the amp-hour capacities add together. Use this to figure out the

Six, 4-volt 1325 AH batteries wired in series to produce 24 volts.

best combination of strings (series) of batteries running parallel to each other. For instance, let's say our daily watt-hour requirement is 1,500 and we want to store power for four days (6,000 watt-hours). Multiply that by two to ensure we don't over-discharge our batteries (12,000 watt-hours). The temperature will drop to 70 degrees overnight, so we correct for that (12,000 watt-hours × 1.04 = 12,480 watt-hours). It's a 12V system, so 12,480/12 = 1,040. That's the amp-hour capacity our battery bank needs. We have chosen a deep-cycle battery with 105 amp-hour capacity, which means we'll need ten of them wired in parallel.

Sizing the Solar Module Array

Actually, modifying this formula to other charging devices (generators, micro-hydro, wind) is easy. Just figure the total amp-hours needed per day, and get devices that provide it to your battery bank.

Step 1. Divide watts per day by the system voltage to figure the total amp-hours needed per day.

Step 2. Multiply the figure by 1.2 to account for battery loss.

Step 3 (for solar). On a solar insolation chart or map, find the average hours of sun per day for your area. (I like the maps rather than the charts; try http://howto.altenergystore.com/ Solar-Insolation-Map-USA/a44/ or http://www. solar4power.com/solar-power-insolation-window .html).

Step 4. Divide the figure from line 2 by the solar insolation number from Step 3. This will give you the amps needed.

Step 5. Determine the peak amperage produced by your solar panel. To do so, divide the panel's wattage by the peak power point voltage (usually 17 to 17.5 watts).

Step 6. Divide peak amps (Step 5) into total array amps (Step 4). Round to the next highest number. This is the number of panels you'll need if wired in parallel.

Step 7. In this chart, find the number of modules in each series string:

Battery voltage	# modules in each series string
12V	1
24V	2
48V	4

Step 8. Multiply the number of modules in each series string (Step 7) by the total number of modules needed if wired in parallel (Step 6). This will be the number of modules you'll need to satisfy the amp-hour requirements.

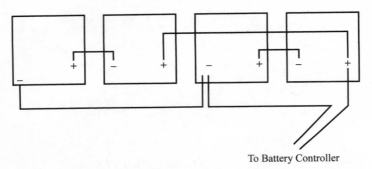

To Battery Controller

An array of two series strings wired in parallel.

Choosing a Solar Panel Mount System

Most mounts are fixed (stationary), some are movable, and others track the sun. Tracking mounts are considered by many to be far from cost-efficient and prone to maintenance problems, and we won't discuss them in detail here. Fixed mounts include pole-top or pole-side mounts, rail mounts, roof mounts, ground mounts, and flush mounts.

Pole-Top (or Pole-Side) Mounts

Pole-top mounts are anchored in the ground, in a hole filled with concrete. The diameter of the hole should be about 2 feet, or for larger poles, 2 feet plus the pole diameter. The hole needs to be half as deep as the height top of the pole above the ground (example: a 6-foot-high

Pole-mounted panels powering billboard lights.

pole should be 9 feet long, with 3 feet embedded in the ground).

Pole-top mounts are easy to install, adjust, and clean, and they keep the panels off the ground and away from shadows formed by shrubbery and curious animals.

When you install post or ground mounts, consider how high they are and how far away they are from obstructions that will cast shadows. If you're mounting the array in summer, remember that the sun is lower in the southern sky in the winter, and there may be 20 or more feet of additional northerly shadow in winter.

Pole-side mounts can hold several panels and are mounted to the pole with hose clamps or u-bolts. The more panels you have, the thicker the pole must be. The racks are designed with either a mid-range fixed position or with an adjustable position for the best angle to the sun.

Install a pole that's big enough to add onto as your system grows.

Rail Mounts

This term generally refers to the rail-like structural piece that the panel is mounted on rather than the location where it's placed. Rail mounts can be rooftop arrays on metal tracks or boat arrays mounted on the boats rails. Some rail mounts are tilted racks leaning against a building, or freestanding ones, set apart from the building. There are even rail mounts for poles. The idea with many rail mounts is similar to that of the adjustable luggage rack on the top of an SUV.

Roof Mounts

Roof mounts take up unused space and can look very tidy, but they do have some problems. First, to adjust the angle or clean them, you have to get up on the roof, and that can be a problem when it's covered with ice and snow. Second, the panels are subject to wind,

Adjustable head for pole-mounting of solar panel.

which can cause roof damage at the mounts. In addition to a rack, a roof mount may require legs to adjust the tilt of the panel for maximum exposure to the sun. A roof mount should have at least 6 inches of clearance between the panel and the roof for ventilation.

Ground Mounts

Many ground mounts are virtually the same as roof mounts and can, in fact, be used for either. Some roof-ground mounts can even be used on the side of the building. Other ground mounts resemble an A-frame and are used only on the ground. Ground mounts are usually well secured to a cement slab or other heavy earth anchor.

Flush Mounts

Flush mounts are commonly used for single panels or very small arrays, typically on RVs and boats. They usually consist of little more than some type of end bracket screwed to the panel frame and bolted onto the roof. They usually have no tilt adjustment, but are inexpensive and easy to install.

Sizing Your Wiring

In normal house wiring, 120 or 240 volts AC wiring is sized for safe ampacity (amperage carrying capacity) to prevent fires. Lower-voltage DC systems are wired for both ampacity and to prevent power loss. The size of electrical wire needs to be large enough to carry all the current produced without too much voltage loss. Voltage drops can cause serious inefficiencies in low-voltage systems

Flush mounts on an Airstream.

(12V or less) because there are so few volts to start with. A voltage drop of 1 volt in a 12-volt system results in ten times the loss of power that would be experienced with a 1V drop in a 120V system. In your low-voltage DC system the drop between PV modules and the battery bank should not exceed 2 percent (0.24V), and between the battery bank and the working circuits should not exceed 5 percent (0.6V).

There are wire sizing charts in any book about alternative electricity sources, and if you type the words "solar wire sizing" into your search engine, you will come up with hundreds of sites that will explain voltage loss.

These sites will walk you through the same charts we have here, or through charts for specific voltage losses.

> *Step 1.* Let's start with what's called the VDI, or voltage drop index, which is a number based on the resistance of wire. The VDI is calculated by multiplying the distance in feet of the wire by the acceptable percentage of voltage drop:
>
> VDI = (amps × distance) / (% loss × voltage)
>
> *Step 2.* Find your VDI in the following chart and find its corresponding AWG (American Wire Gauge) and ampacity. You must not exceed the ampacity given for the AWG wire size.

If you need to determine the required metric size (instead of AWG) for copper wire, multiply the VDI by 1.1, and for aluminum wire multiply the VDI by 1.7 to get the required cross-sectional metric size.

Example: A 15-ampere load at 12V over 50 feet of copper with a 2 percent loss:

VDI = (15x50/2x12) = 31.25. The nearest VDI is 31, requiring AWG 2.

Note that with AWG gauges, the higher the number, the thinner the wire.

AWG Wire Size	Area mm²	Copper VDI - Ampacity	Aluminium VDI - Ampacity
16	1.31	1 - 10	Not recommended
14	2.08	2 - 15	Not recommended
12	3.31	3 - 20	Not recommended
10	5.26	5 - 30	Not recommended
8	8.37	8 - 55	Not recommended
6	13.3	12 - 75	Not recommended
4	21.1	20 - 95	Not recommended
2	33.6	31 - 130	20 - 100
0	53.5	49 - 170	31 - 132
00	67.4	62 - 195	39 - 150
000	85.0	78 - 225	49 - 175
0000	107	99 - 260	62 - 205

Turbine and generator setup near electrical shed
at the Valley of Gods B&B.

Appendix 5
A Look at Biodigestors
by Arlene Foss

Biodigestors are still a relatively new concept for most, especially in the First World. However, for many years, rural families around the world, especially in countries like Asia, India, Philippines, Mexico, Central, and South America, have constructed systems to convert accessible animal and/or plant waste into gas fuel (biogas) for household use, i.e., for stoves, lamps, hot-water tanks.

Biodigestors function using an anaerobic process of decomposition/composting/fermentation, where the bacteria in the manure or plant compost produce a mixture of methane, carbon dioxide, and small amount of other gases.

Biodigestors are relatively simple and inexpensive to build and maintain. Operation entails little more than a steady supply of an organic matter and water mixture.

What is biogas?

Biogas is a fuel gas that is produced by the anaerobic digestion of organic material, mostly methane, and is often called "marsh gas" or "swamp gas" because it is also produced by the same process that occurs during the underwater decomposition of organic material in wetland areas.

BENEFITS

- *Reduces the amount of wood (and work involved to collect that wood) or other more expensive and/or polluting fuels already in use.*

- *Increased preservation of forest areas in environments where communities use wood as the primary fuel. In turn the quality of water, air, and animal/plant habitats that the forests provide are maintained.*

- *Produces a very high nutrient-rich organic fertilizer as a by-product, thanks to the bacterial activity and anaerobic environment. In turn, reduces the use of chemical fertilizer (a toxin affecting ground, water, plants, and the food we eat) and again in turn, saving farmers money.*

- *In many places, improves household air quality by reducing dependence on woodstoves and in turn decreases health problems related to smoke and fire.*

- *Provides a method to treat raw waste into recycled, usable, inexpensive fuel that would normally directly contaminate ground and water entering into clean streams, lakes, and rivers.*
- *Reduces illnesses caused by contamination, as well as fly and mosquito populations.*
- *Reduces greenhouse gas emissions of CO_2 and methane.*

Feedstock

To produce an organic fertilizer by-product, organic matter that is pesticide- and chemical-free must be used as well. Starchy and sugary refuse ferments very well. Dung from cattle, horses, sheep, pigs, and even humans, or any biodegradable compostable waste works well. Pig manure, especially corn- or grain-fed animals (starchy), works better than cow, due to the fact that cow manure is already more digested. The effluent or by-product of a biodigestor can be used in fish ponds to produce aquatic plants. Aquatic plants produce material to feed animals and/or to make compost. Some plant materials contain a lot of cellulose and lignins which are not easily digestible in a biodigestors.

Size of Biodigestor System

The size of a family biodigestor depends on:

- the number of family members using the gas;
- how much usage is desired for cooking, lighting, hot water per day; and
- how much organic waste is readily and regularly available.

Producing Gas

Gas can be produced in as early as 30 days, or in up to 70 days, depending on:

- type of feedstock used;
- climate temperatures;
- the presence of bacteria (which is required);
- proper maintenance of the anaerobic environment inside the biodigestor; and
- maintaining as close to a neutral pH balance as possible to allow for anaerobic process.

Temperature

The warmer the ambient environment climate, the better and faster the biogas-producing process works.

Fermentation needs heat and ideally a temperature of 30 to 38 degrees Celsius (86 to 100 degrees Fahrenheit). Some climates have dramatic changes from season to season and/or from day to night.

Practicality

A biodigestor will work well for you if you have these components:

- Animals of sufficient quantity to "power" a biodigestor.
- Enough warm climate and/or the ability to build a heated shelter surrounding the system.
- Adaptations to use biogas in your home (lamps, stoves, hot-water tank).
- Space enough to construct a system of your required size.

Cost

Depending on the size of the biodigestors and the type or style of materials one chooses to use—from using even some recycled plastic containers to making some of the parts, to something more elaborate—the cost could vary from $600 and up, and, of course, depending on the country in which one buys these materials.

The budget available will somewhat dictate the type of materials chosen as well.

Biodigestors are being built and used on a commercial basis as well, where waste material from huge feedlots and/or other large waste producers can be used on a grander scale.

Biogas technology can improve life, save money, and increase productivity of a farm, and at the same time help to protect our natural resources.

—Contributed by ARLENE FOSS. She wrote this chapter upon returning home to Canada after several years of humanitarian work in Chiapas, Mexico, where she was involved in a biogas project.

Glossary

A

accumulator: A battery that can be recharged (e.g., the lead-acid battery in your car).

active system: A system that uses moving parts to perform its function. An *active solar system* uses pumps, controls, and power while solar energy is being harvested.

air lock: The space between two doors to keep weather from entering inside.

alternating current (AC): Current that changes its direction of flow (polarity) 60 times per second; usually 120 or 240 volts in North America; easy to transmit, but cannot be stored except by converting it to DC (direct current).

alternative energy: Various energies produced from nontraditional methods, i.e., photovoltaic, wind, micro-hydro.

alternator: A generator that produces alternating current.

ambient: Prevailing outdoor conditions, generally of wind or temperature.

amorphous silicon: A photovoltaic cell made without a crystalline structure.

ampere (amp): The unit of measurement of electrical current.

amp-hour: A unit of measure of a quantity of electrical current per hour (1 amp per 1 hour).

angle of incidence: The angle at which sunlight hits a flat surface.

anode: The positive pole or point of entry of electric current; the positive electrode of a battery cell.

antifreeze: A chemical compound that stops fluids from freezing.

aquifer: An underground layer of porous rock or unconsolidated sediment containing water and into which a well can be sunk.

armature: An iron core wound with wire (a coil) that is turned through a magnetic field to produce alternating current.

array: An orderly grouping (e.g., solar panel array).

array current: The amperage produced by an array of solar modules in full sunlight.

azimuth: The angle measured horizontally and clockwise from true north (north being 0 degrees, and south, 180 degrees).

B

backup: A secondary energy source that backs up the primary source when it is inadequate or fails.

ballast: A device used to provide the starting voltage or to stabilize the current in a circuit; commonly used for fluorescent and compact fluorescent-type bulbs.

baseload: The minimum load of electrical power needed to maintain continuous operation at the time of lowest demand.

battery: A series of cells that store electrical energy. Each cell converts chemical energy into electricity or vice versa.

battery bank: A group of batteries connected together using series or parallel wiring.

battery capacity: The maximum amount of amp-hours possible to draw from a fully charged battery over a certain period of time.

battery life cycle: The number of operating cycles a battery can sustain before failing.

berm: A man-made hill.

black water: Sewage water from domestic toilets.

blocking diode: An electrical part that prevents loss of energy to an inactive array of photovoltaic modules.

BTU (British Thermal Unit): The amount of heat needed to increase the temperature of 1 pound of water by 1 degree Fahrenheit (3,411 BTUs = 1 kilowatt-hour).

bus bar: Usually a metal bar using connections to where all energy sources and loads connect to each other;

main power terminal to which circuits are attached through either fuses or circuit breakers.

C

carbon footprint: The direct effect our actions and lifestyles have on the environment in terms of carbon dioxide emissions.

cathode: A negative electrode (negative pole) in a battery.

cell: A unit or module assembly for storing or harvesting energy (e.g., solar cell) or for generating electricity (e.g., battery cell that generates electricity by chemical reactions); the smallest structural unit capable of independent generation of electricity (e.g., the cells within solar modules or batteries).

CF (compact fluorescent): A lightbulb using an integral ballast; small fluorescent bulbs which have built-in ballasts and medium screw bases for replacement of incandescent bulbs.

charge controller: A mechanism used to manage the rate and state of charge of a series of batteries. Related terms:

activation voltage: voltage at which a charge controller will take action to protect the batteries

adjustable set point: permits adjustment of voltage disconnect levels

cut-in: the point when a control device connects its target device

cut-off voltage (aka, low-voltage cut-off): the voltage level where the array is set to disconnect from the load from the battery or the array from the battery

cut-out: the point when a control interrupts an action

high-voltage disconnect: the level of battery voltage to which a charge controller is set to disconnect the batteries from the array to prevent overcharging

low-voltage disconnect: the voltage to which the controller is set to disconnect the load from the battery

low-voltage warning: a light or buzzer to indicate low battery voltage

maximum power tracking: a circuit that maintains voltage of an array of batteries at maximum current flow

multistage controller: a device that provides multilevel control of the charging and loading of batteries

reverse current protection: prevents current from flowing from battery to the array

single-stage controller: a device that only has a single level of control to manage charging or loading

temperature compensation: allowance made in the charge controller set points to allow a charging battery to match ambient temperature in order to optimize a charge

charge rate: The rate (ratio of battery capacity to charging current flow) at which a battery is recharged.

chemical energy: Energy stored in a substance and released during chemical reactions.

circuit: Continuous pathway for current flow from a power source to an appliance or device.

compost: Decaying organic matter.

concentrator: A mirror or lens-like part of a photovoltaic array that concentrates sun rays onto smaller cells to improve energy output.

conductance: The ability of a substance to allow electricity or heat to pass through it.

conduction: The transfer of heat within a material without any motion of the object or material.

conductor: A substance through which an electrical current or heat will flow.

convection: The transfer of heat by the motion of a fluid or gas to regions of different temperature.

convection current: The circuit of fluid or gas circulation caused by convection.

conversion efficiency: The ratio (percentage) of energy input (store) to actual output.

cross-ventilation: Various openings in a structure to allow air to pass through.

crystalline silicon: The material that most photovoltaic cells are made from. *Single crystalline* and *polycrystalline* are two common materials used for producing solar cells.

current: The movement of electrons from an area of high electric potential (too many electrons) to an area of low potential (not enough electrons). Current is measured in amperes ("amps").

cycle: The process of discharging a fully charged battery and then fully recharging it again.

D

days of autonomy (storage): The amount of time in days that a storage system is able to supply the normal amount of energy needed without having to replenish.

deep-cycle battery: A type of battery created to handle many cycles of deep discharge of 50 percent or more of its total capacity.

depth of discharge (DOD): The amount (percentage) of rated energy capacity withdrawn from a battery.

diode: A component which allows electricity to travel in one direction only.

direct current (DC): Electrical current that flows only in one direction, from one pole to another.

discharge: The draw of energy from a storage system.

discharge rate: The rate in amps or time that electrical current is taken from a battery.

disconnect: A type of control used for interrupting or completing an electrical flow between units.

dopant (doping): Tiny and minutely regulated amount of specific chemicals added to a semiconductor matrix to control the density and probable flow of free electrons.

dry cell: A battery with sealed compartments containing electrolyte paste.

duty cycle: The ratio between active time and total time, used in describing PV systems.

duty rating: The amount of time a component can be operated at full capacity before failure can be expected.

E

earth shelter: A structure burrowed into a south-facing slope with the north side buried in the earth.

earthship: A structure built with tires packed full of earth (rammed earth).

efficiency: The percentage of actual measure to the theoretical optimum.

electrode: A terminal of an electric circuit; a terminal by which electric current enters or leaves a battery or electric energy-harvesting device.

electrolyte: The chemical, usually a liquid, in a battery that transfers the electrical charge between positive and negative electrodes.

electromagnet: A wire wrapped around an iron bar. When current is passed through the wire, the bar behaves like a bar magnet.

electron: A negatively charged particle that exists around the nucleus of an atom.

energy density: The ratio of stored energy to the weight or volume of storage.

energy-efficient: Using energy to accomplish a task in a way that there is little waste of that energy or time.

Energy Guide label: The yellow label on the back of a new appliance that compares its energy efficiency with similar models.

ENERGY STAR: A voluntary EPA program to identify energy-efficient appliances with the goal of reducing greenhouse gas emissions from power plants.

equalizing: An occasional overcharging of batteries to ensure all cells continue to reach an acceptable rate of charge.

evapotranspiration: The loss of moisture through the combination of evaporation from wet soil and transpiration ("breathing") from plants.

F

fail-safe: The design of a system that will force it into a safe mode without damage, in the event of a failure.

float charge: A charge given to a battery equal to or somewhat more than its natural tendency to self-discharge.

frequency: The measure in number of peaks in a section of a wave; 1 unit = Hertz per second.

G

gassing (outgassing): The process of gas being given off when batteries are charging.

generator: A device that converts the energy of magnetic movement into electricity.

glazing: Glass, usually window glass. High-tech glass is commonly made of two sheets (panes) sealed together with the inner space filled with an inert gas such as krypton or argon, and sometimes a plastic membrane or a tint is added.

gravity-fed: When the weight of water provides enough pressure by the storage tank being placed high enough above the point of use.

gray water: Household wastewater from shower and kitchen; any wastewater other than sewage.

green: Products made from recycled materials; materials that have a decreased impact on the environment because of durability (less throw-away); materials made from or reliant on renewable resources; products manufactured efficiently with minimal energy use and using raw materials; using nontoxic and nonpolluting materials; using sustainable materials and energy.

greenhouse gases: Gases such as carbon dioxide and methane trapped in the atmosphere that prevent heat energy from escaping from the earth in the same way glass prevents heat from escaping from a greenhouse.

grid: A distribution network of transmission power or water lines from various sources throughout a large area.

grid-connected system: Residential, business, or other electrical system that draws energy from the grid.

groundwater: Water runoff onto open ground from precipitation or other sources.

ground wire: Usually a bare copper wire used as a safety device that provides a path to the ground through which current can escape.

H

head: In a hydroelectric system, the distance water falls from the collector to the turbine.

heat exchanger: A mechanism that transfers heat derived from one source to another system; a device that transfers heat through a conducting wall from one fluid to another.

high-tech glass: Glass windows for buildings made of two sheets of glass hermetically sealed together with the inner space filled with an inert gas and sometimes a plastic membrane.

HVAC (space conditioning): Heating, ventilation, and air-conditioning of internal areas of structures.

hydroelectricity: Electricity generated when moving water turns a turbine.

hydrometer: An instrument used to measure the specific gravity of a substance.

I

incandescent bulb: An energy-intensive lightbulb that uses electricity to heat a filament until photons are emitted to produce light.

infiltration: Ambient outside air entering a house through wall cracks and rendering space conditioning a waste.

infrared: Light that exists just outside the visible spectrum and will radiate heat.

infrastructure: Aspects of civilization that are used to function in daily life (i.e., roads, water systems, power, phone services, fire departments, public health services, school systems, government programs, garbage disposal).

insolation (incident solar radiation): The amount of sunlight falling on an area; irradiance over a given time.

insulation: A material that inhibits energy from transferring from one place to another.

insulator: A substance that cannot conduct a current of electricity.

Integrated Collector Storage (ICS): The combination of solar collector and storage tank in one unit.

interconnect (intertie): To make an electrical connection between two systems, a power producer and distribution lines on a grid, in a way that each can draw from or supply to each other.

intertie: A power generation system that makes it possible to generate your own power and to sell the excess back to the power company.

internal energy: The kinetic energy plus the potential energy of the atoms a substance is made of.

inverter: A device that changes direct current (DC) to alternating current (AC).

irradiance: The direct, diffuse, and reflected solar radiation that strikes a surface, usually expressed in kilowatts per square meter.

J

joule (J): The unit in which energy or work is measured.

junction: A transitional border between semiconductor layers, such as a p/n junction, which goes from a high concentration of acceptors (P-type) to a high concentration of donors (N-type).

K

kilowatt: A measure of instantaneous work; 1,000 watts = 1 kilowatt.

kilowatt-hour: The standard unit of power usage.

kinetic energy: The energy of movement.

L

landfill: An open ground pit where refuse is dumped and generally covered over.

Law of Conservation of Energy: A law of physics which states that energy cannot be destroyed or created but can change its form.

lead-acid: The standard household and automotive battery.

LED (light-emitting diode): A very efficient type of electrical light.

life: In terms of electrical systems, the period of time that function or specified performance can be expected.

line-tied system: An electrical system that is connected to a power line generally having domestic power-generating capability with the ability to return power to the grid as well as to draw from it, depending on load and generator status.

load: Amount of energy used by an electrical device; an appliance or device that consumes electricity by converting it to other forms of energy such as heat, sound, or light.

load circuit: The wiring that provides the pathway for the current that is used by an electrical device.

load current (in amps): The amount of electrical current needed to operate a device.

low voltage: Another term for 12- or 24-volt DC.

M

magnetic field: The area around a magnet in which a magnetic force operates.

maintenance-free battery: An enclosed battery unit to which water cannot be added (even though all batteries need routine inspection).

maximum power point tracking (MPPT): The point to which a power-changing device continuously controls photovoltaic voltage received from the source in order to maintain it at its maximum output current.

microclimate: Long-term weather trends or conditions of a small area, even as small as a domestic garden.

micro-hydro: Energy generated from a small waterfall system.

milliamp: One thousandth of one ampere.

module: A manufactured panel generally containing 36 photovoltaic cells within an aluminum frame, covered with glass or acrylic, wiring, and a junction box to connect between itself, more modules, and the system.

mulch: Natural compost (e.g., topsoil from the forest).

N

NEC (National Electrical Code): Guidelines set out for all forms of electrical installations.

net metering: A desirable type of "buy-back" agreement where the power meter of a house that is line-tied calculates in the favor of the utility company when grid power is being drawn, but then in the homeowner's favor when his power generation exceeds his needs; then, power flows back to the grid. When the power bill is due, the meter is read; then, the homeowner is either credited or charged according to the net metering.

NiCad (nickel cadmium): A form of chemical storage used by some rechargeable batteries.

nominal voltage: The terminal voltage of a battery or cell, discharged at a specific rate and temperature, usually measured in multiples of 12.

nonrenewable energy: Energy that can only be used once.

normal operating cell temperature: Standard operating temperature of a PV module in its working environment.

N-type silicon: Doped silicon that contains more electrons than simple silicon, therefore having a net negative charge.

O

off-grid: Not connected to grid transmission lines and being energy self-sufficient.

off-peak energy: Utility companies generally need to keep their generators running and need to sell the abundance of energy during baseload periods; usually will sell cheaper than during the regular periods.

ohm: The unit of resistance to an electrical current.

on-grid: Being connected to the expansive grid network of electrical distribution lines (or other types of grid lines, such as water).

online: Ready to operate and connected to the system.

open-circuit voltage: Maximum amount of voltage that can be measured from a PV cell, module, or array without carrying a load.

orientation: A position in relation to the four cardinal directions: north, south, east, and west (*azimuth* is the measure of orientation).

outgas: The giving off of gases from any material.

overcharge: Forcing additional current into an already fully charged battery.

overcurrent: A dangerous overload of current for the rating of wiring (circuit breakers and fuses create an interruption to prevent this from happening).

P

panel: A flat modular structure; a surface within a compartment.

parallel: Connecting positive poles to positive poles in an electrical circuit, and negative to negative, which raises the current without affecting the voltage.

particulates: Particles so tiny that they continue to suspend themselves in the air or water.

passive solar: Comfortable space conditioning by using and retaining solar heat.

passive system: A system that uses no moving parts.

passively heated: Sole use of the sun's rays for heating energy.

pathogen: A microorganism (bacteria, virus, etc.) capable of causing disease.

peak demand: The time in a day or year when users require the largest amount of electricity.

peak kilowatt: A unit of power used during peak demand periods for which customers are usually charged the highest price.

peak load: The maximum load required of a single system.

peak sun hours: The equal amount of hours per day that solar irradiance averages "one sun."

peak watt: The laboratory-determined measure of the optimum output of a module.

Pelton wheel: A special turbine that converts flowing water into rotational energy.

phantom loads: Energy used by appliances (i.e., a microwave with a clock) that continue to use power even when not in use.

PHEV: Plug-in hybrid electric vehicle.

photon: The theoretical particle used to describe light.

photovoltaics: Modules or cells that are exposed to the sun's rays to generate electricity.

plates: Thin, flat pieces of material inside a battery, usually metal, used to collect electrical energy.

plug-loads: Appliances or any electrical unit plugged into a power system.

PN-junction: The plane in a PV cell where positive and negative doped silicon layers join.

pollution: Dumping of any toxic or unnatural materials into the air, water, or onto the ground.

potential difference: Electrical pressure (similar to water pressure); the energy needed to push a certain amount of electric charge along a conducting pathway between two points; the difference between two points, one of which has too many electrons, and the other not enough, causing current to flow between them. Potential difference is measured in volts.

potential energy: The energy an object has due to its position in a force field.

power: The rate at which kinetic energy is produced or used; energy that performs work; measured in watts. In electronics, power is the product of voltage (potential difference) multiplied by amperage (current).

power conditioning equipment: Electrical units that alter forms of electricity (e.g., inverter) or other types that determine the electrical current is reliable and ensure that it is of the correct form for the appliance connected to it (e.g., surge protector).

power density: Ratio of the rated power available to the weight or volume of a battery.

power supply: A device that converts one form of electricity to another and distributes it (e.g., rectifiers and inverters).

P-type silicon: A silicon material that has too few electrons and thus has a net positive charge.

PURPA (Public Utility Regulatory Policy Act): A 1978 federal legislation, part of the National Energy Act, that required utility companies to purchase power from anyone at the utility company's avoided cost.

PVs: Photovoltaics.

R

radiation: The transfer of heat by electromagnetic waves traveling away from the heat source.

rated battery capacity: The standard specified rate that the maximum energy can be drawn from a battery.

rated module current: The lab-tested indication of PV module current, determined by the manufacturer.

rectifier: A device used on DC generators to convert AC to DC to distribute it to a battery bank.

renewable energy: An energy source that is produced faster than we can use it.

resistance: The ability of a substance to resist the flow of electricity, measured in ohms.

retrofit: To install new equipment in a place not originally designed for it.

RPM (rotations per minute): Rate at which a motor or wheel turns.

R-value: Resistance value, a factor used specifically to rate insulation materials. The rating is used to measure the material's resistance to heat flow. The higher it is, the more effective it is. In the U.S. the average recommended R-value in a warm environment is R-35 in ceilings and R-18 in walls. In cold environments it's R-44 in ceilings and R20 in walls.

S

secondary battery: A battery that can be discharged and recharged fully.

self-discharge: A battery's tendency to lose its own charge through internal chemical activity.

semiconductor: A material that has a limited ability to conduct electrical current.

septic system: A system using a large tank that collects and releases wastewater.

series connections: Wiring components together with alternating poles (positive to negative, positive to negative), which increases voltage but not current.

set point: The point at which electrical controls are adjusted to change their action.

shallow-cycle battery: A battery that is designed to stay fully charged (i.e., automotive battery).

shelf life: The maximum length of time an item or material can be stored and still be expected to perform to specs.

short circuit: A low-resistance connection between two points in an electric circuit. It may occur by accident or intentionally. The current flows through the area of

low resistance, bypassing the rest of the circuit, and
possibly resulting in a blowout, burn, or sparking.

short-circuit current: The current produced when the
output terminals of a PV cell, module, or array are
connected to each other (short circuit).

silicon: An element, commonly found as quartz sand,
used to make photovoltaic cells.

single crystal silicon: Silicon or sand crystals that are
carefully melted down, grown, sliced, and treated
to create highly effective PV cells.

solar aperture: In the northern hemisphere, the zone
to the south of an area where the sun traverses.
This zone changes with the change of seasons and
when objects such as trees, buildings, or mountains narrow this field.

solar cell: Photovoltaic cell; a cell that turns solar energy
into electricity.

solar collector: A device used to turn solar energy into
heat energy in order to heat water.

solar fluid: The fluid used within indirect solar water
heating systems.

solar fraction: The amount of electricity that can
reasonably be expected to be produced from the
amount of sun falling on a particular site, taking into
account solar aperture factors.

solar hot-water heating: The process of using solar
heat, directly or indirectly, to heat water. Solar
heating is done by *indirect systems* (aka, closed-loop

systems) which use a heat transfer fluid in the collector, or by *direct systems* (aka, open-loop systems) which heat the water directly in the collector.

solar oven: Basically a container with a glass front and internal reflectors designed to heat food by using the sun's rays falling on it (electromagnetic radiation).

solar panels: Flat devices set in direct sunlight to harvest its solar energy.

solar photovoltaic principles: Solar principles applied to the production of electricity.

solar resource: The amount of insolation received by an area, calculated in kilowatt-hours per square meter per day.

solar thermal principles: Solar principles applied to the heating of air, fluids, or solids.

solenoid (aka, coil): A coil of wire that creates an electromagnetic field when a current passes through it.

specific gravity: The relative density of a substance (liquid, solid, or gas) compared to air or water.

stand-alone: A system that does not need an outside source of energy; self-sufficient.

standby: A backup device that is kept in reserve for times when a primary system fails.

state of charge: The actual amount (percentage) of energy stored compared to a battery's maximum rated capacity.

stratification: What happens when electrolyte acid concentration in a sedentary battery separates into layers.

subarray: Part of a PV array which is wired to be managed independently.

sulfating: What happens with lead-acid batteries that form lead-sulfate crystals on the plates and leads.

sun-tempered: Structures designed to take simple advantage of the most obvious methods of collecting and using the sun's energy.

surge capacity: The designed ability of a battery or inverter to withstand a quick power surge over and above the rated capacity, to give the required boost a device needs to start.

sustainable: Energy sources, resources, or materials that are required and used on a regular basis, which when managed carefully to ensure renewability, can continue to be available indefinitely.

T

task lighting: Lighting specific areas while leaving other areas dim or unlit in order to conserve energy.

terminals: Points of electrical contact representing opposite poles (positive and negative).

thermal capacity: A material's ability to absorb heat.

thermal mass: The solid volume of a structure that absorbs heat; when the ambient temperature falls, the absorbed heat then radiates outward.

thermoelectric: Having to do with the heat produced by electricity.

thermopane: A method of window construction that reduces the loss or gain of heat from a structure.

thermosiphon: A circulation system based on the fact that warmer substances rise; by placing the solar energy collector below the hot-water tank system, hot-water circulation is automatic.

tilt angle: The angle of a panel measured from the horizontal.

tracker: A mechanism that tracks the sun and keeps the panel perpendicular to it.

transformer: An electrical device that changes alternating current (AC) voltage.

trickle charge: A small current intended to keep a battery in full charge when not in use.

true solar: A structure design that makes maximum use of south-side window space, insulation, and thermal mass.

tungsten filament: The tiny coil in a lightbulb that glows hot and bright when electricity passes through it.

turbine: A vaned or paddled wheel that turns rapidly when fast-moving water or wind is passed over it, converting flow energy into rotational energy.

U

ultrafilter: Removes impurities and particulates of submicron size, i.e., Giardia and larger viruses.

uninterruptible power supply (UPS): An energy system device that provides reliable temporary backup power output for critical uses.

V

varistor: A voltage-dependent variable resistor that is used to protect sensitive equipment from power spikes (e.g., lightning) and diverts unwanted energy to the ground.

vented cell: A vent mechanism designed into a battery cell with intent to expel gases during charging.

volt: A unit of measure of the potential difference between two points in an electrical circuit.

voltage drop: Voltage potential decrease over a long distance due to the wire's resistance.

W

water catchment system: Where groundwater resources are poor, this system can be used to capture and store precipitation and runoff.

water table: The underground surface below which the soil is saturated with water.

watt: The unit with which power is measured; the rate of performing work.

watt-hour: The total amount of power used or produced in one hour; the amount of work done (1 watt per 1 hour).

waveform: The trace of voltage characteristics of an alternating current (AC) over time as viewed on an oscilloscope.

well: A hole dug to the water table or aquifer.

wet shelf life: The length of time that a charged electrolyte-filled battery can sit unused before falling below its minimal performance level.

wind chill: A temperature equivalent calculated using ambient temperature and wind speed. Wind makes temperatures feel colder.

wind farm: A set of individual wind turbines for generating electricity.

X

xeriscaping: A method of landscaping to conserve water.

Y

yurt: A westernized Asian word that refers to traditional nomadic round dwellings.

INDEX